Crafting with Cookie Molds
Polymer Clay Mixed Media Projects to Beautify Your Home, Give as Gifts, and Celebrate the Holidays

— Anne L. Watson —

It's a match! Cookie molds and polymer clay are perfect crafting companions!

So says Anne L. Watson, whose earlier books helped spark a cookie molds revival. As Anne has discovered, cookie dough and polymer clay have a lot in common, and a mold made for one will work brilliantly with the other. The mold does the main work of shaping the clay, making you look like an expert every time! And many cookie molds are "bakeable," so that figures come out of the mold perfectly formed and already hardened.

Besides that, contemporary cookie molds come in shapes, patterns, and themes that will appeal to polymer clay and mixed media crafters as well as cookie bakers. So, while bakers will find a new use for their molds, crafters will discover countless new designs to grace their projects.

Crafting with Cookie Molds includes everything you need to get started: basic tips and techniques, plus over thirty of Anne's own decorative projects, from beginning to advanced, illustrated with over 170 photos. You'll find Christmas tree ornaments, boxes, baskets, shelf standers, wreaths, gingerbread houses, and more. And if you want to use the very same cookie molds as Anne, they're identified by maker, with notes on where to find them.

Welcome to the exciting new world of polymer clay and cookie molds!

"Charming . . . Watson offers a thorough introduction to a clever new craft . . . A comprehensive, organized, and deliciously readable manual that provides instruction with enthusiasm and ease."

Kirkus Reviews

Books by Anne L. Watson

Cookie Molds
Baking with Cookie Molds
Cookie Molds Around the Year
Crafting with Cookie Molds

Soap and Lotion Making
Smart Soapmaking
Milk Soapmaking
Smart Lotionmaking
Castile Soapmaking
Cool Soapmaking
Smart Soapmaking Around the Year

Lifestyle
Smart Housekeeping
Smart Housekeeping Around the Year
Living Apart Together

CRAFTING WITH
Cookie Molds

Polymer Clay Mixed Media Projects to Beautify Your Home, Give as Gifts, and Celebrate the Holidays

Anne L. Watson

Photos by Aaron Shepard

Shepard Publications
Bellingham, Washington

**For more treats and resources, as well as
personal answers to your questions,
visit Anne's Cookie Molds Page at**

www.annelwatson.com/cookiemolds

Contents

Part 2—Projects

Baskets

Page 25

Page 27

Boxes and Canisters

Page 30

Page 35

Table Decorations

Page 39

Page 41

Shelf and Counter Decorations

CONTENTS

Wall and Door Decorations

Page 51

Page 53

Other Room Decorations

Christmas Projects

Page 58

Page 62

Page 63

Page 67

Saint Nicholas Shelf Stander (page 58)

A Good Start

"Too pretty to eat!"

If you make molded cookies, you've heard that one over and over. And if you're like me, you don't know what to say. It's a compliment, but it can also feel frustrating.

If all your work and skill gives you cookies that can't be eaten, what are you supposed to do with them? Make decorations? Hang them on the wall? Display them on a shelf?

Well, yes, that's *exactly* what you can do—if you make molded "cookies" out of polymer clay.

"Cookies" like that can decorate a holiday tree or a wreath. They can adorn a box, a basket, a canister, a candlestick, or any number of other gifts, prized possessions, or common household items. They can even stand on their own, as when made into a planter box or a gingerbread house.

Of course, not everyone reading this book has ever made a molded cookie. Maybe instead you're experienced in mixed media or polymer clay, and you're looking for new directions for your craft. Or maybe, as a beginner, you love that a cookie mold could do the hardest part of shaping clay, leaving you to reap the rewards!

As I've discovered, molds designed for cookie dough are also well suited to polymer clay, with its similar consistency. For instance, unlike some other mold types, cookie molds avoid spindly elements that might cause trouble in a polymer clay figure. And many cookie molds are "bakeable," making it easy for you to form and unmold a perfect clay image.

What's more, molds made for cookie bakers are available with many shapes, patterns, and themes appealing to polymer clay and mixed media crafters as well. You'll find there are countless unique and beautiful items you can make with them, opening up a whole new world to explore.

Whichever side you're coming from—cookie molds or crafts—this book will get you off to a good start combining them. Part 1 will give you the basics on tools, supplies, and general methods—most of what you'll need to make the projects in this book or other projects like them.

It's likely you already have most or all of the essential tools and supplies—craft knives, scissors, baking parchment, cornstarch, things like that. Along with such rock bottom necessities, I list things that are optional but helpful.

None of my general methods are hard, though some require time and patience. Still, there are some easy things I had to learn the hard way, and there are other things I've worked out to solve the problems of other crafters. My directions will save you the time and trouble of figuring out everything for yourself.

Part 2 is projects of my own that I've enjoyed making and displaying. For those who want to replicate my pieces closely, I've made the directions as thorough and detailed as I can, and also identified the makers of the more important molds.

Or you can use the projects as a starting point to design something different. You might want to use different molds than I did, or even the same molds in different ways. Or just let my piece provide a spark for a creation entirely your own.

The possibilities are endless. About the only thing you *can't* do with polymer clay "cookies" is eat them!

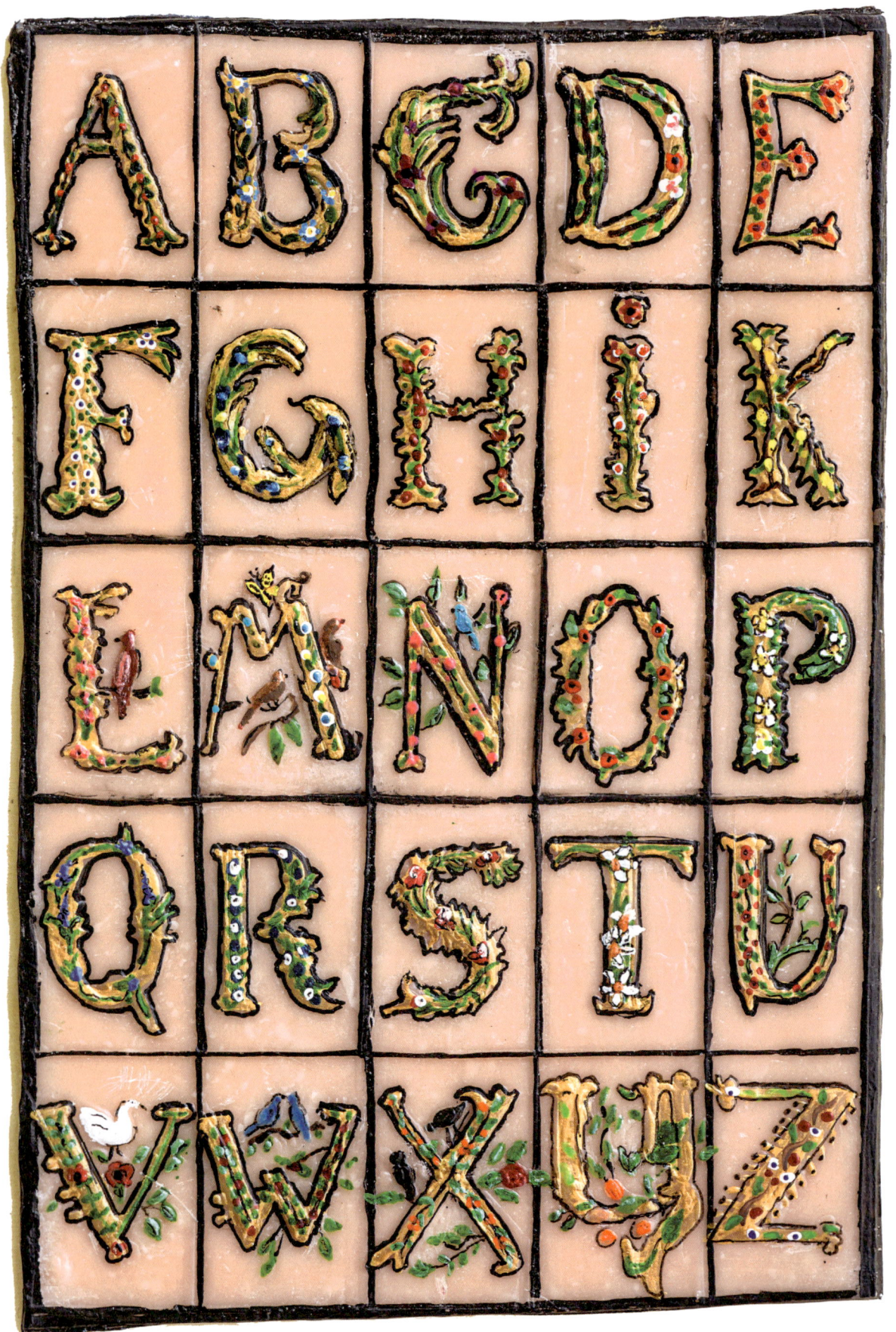

Detail of Alphabet Bookend (page 45)

Part 1
Basics

 # Basic Tools

Here are tools you'll generally want on hand for the kinds of projects in this book. Other tools, more useful for individual projects, will be listed with those.

Preferences in tools are fairly personal, so you may have items you want to add to my list, or I may list items you won't find especially helpful.

Cookie Molds

As you might imagine, the main tool you need for cookie mold crafting is a cookie mold! Molds for my projects are listed with their makers when I think it would be worth seeking out the one I used. Other molds are more generic, so you don't need to worry about finding particular ones.

For working with polymer clay, the most important thing to know about a mold is what it's made from. With some molds, you can bake the clay right in them. In others, you must remove the clay before baking it, or just use air-dry clay. (I'll describe each of these methods in detail.)

Pottery or terra-cotta. You can bake clay in any of these molds.

Silicone. Some silicone molds can withstand baking temperatures and some can't. Ask the supplier before you try it. If you can't get information, assume you *cannot* bake in it.

Metal. Metal molds can be baked, but I wouldn't try it with antique molds. Many of those contain lead, and baking can produce toxic fumes or even cause the alloy to melt.

DO NOT bake in plastic, composition, wood, or resin molds. If you're not sure what a mold is made of, play it safe. Unmold the clay before baking.

Can you use the same cookie mold for both clay and cookies? Feelings sometimes run high about this. One thing I can tell you is that polymer clay is classed as nontoxic and meets the U.S. Consumer Product Safety Commission's strict regulations for children's toys. Still, caution requires me to give the last word to the clay manufacturers, who all recommend *not* using the same tools for both polymer clay and food.

Though the principal molds for all my projects are cookie molds, I've also used molds meant for sugarcraft, resin, chocolate, and other kinds of moldings. All these molds are inexpensive and easy to use, and you should have no trouble finding ones like them.

Cookie Cutters

For some molds, the maker may offer a dedicated cookie cutter to cut out the shape, in case you don't want to cut it out by hand. Other times, though, you may not need or want to cut out the exact shape at all—you just want to cut around it. For that, you can use a generic square or round cookie cutter of medium size.

Of course, there can also be attractive cutters you want to use on a project for the sake of their own design, apart from cutting out any molding.

Wood

Composition

Pottery

Silicone

Resin

FINDING COOKIE MOLDS AND CUTTERS

In my projects, I've featured molds and cutters by small, artisan makers, as well as by larger, well-known companies. Some of these molds and cutters are easy to find online. Others may no longer be made, and the company itself might be gone, but you can probably buy them used. Check below for help in finding cookie molds and cutters by specific makers.

For more generic molds and cutters, Amazon and Google are both great places to search.

Maker	Availability	Where to Find
Alfred E Knobler	Vintage	Try Etsy or eBay
Änis-Paradies	Current	www.springerle.com
Artesão Cookie Molds	Current	artesaocookiemolds.com
Boston Warehouse	Vintage	Try Etsy or eBay
Brown Bag Cookie Art	Vintage	Try Etsy or eBay
Cookie Cutz	Current	cookiecutz.com
Cotton Press	Vintage	Try Etsy or eBay
D.D. Dillon	Vintage	Try Etsy or eBay
DecoLazer	Current	Try Amazon, Etsy, or eBay
DiamondWoodcomua	Current	Etsy shop
EmlemsSiliconeMoulds	Current	Etsy shop
Hartstone Cookie Molds	Vintage	Try Amazon, Etsy, or eBay
HOBI Cookie Molds	Current	www.cookiemold.com
House on the Hill	Current	www.houseonthehill.net
Juno3DStore	Current	Etsy shop
Kato Baking Supplies	Current	katosupplies.com
Kitchen Vixen	Current	Etsy shop
Laxa Family	Vintage	Try Amazon, Etsy, or eBay
Mood for Wood	Current	moodforwood.pl or Etsy shop
My Cookie Mold	Current	www.mycookiemold.com
OZAOZ	Current	Try Amazon
Pampered Chef	Vintage	Try Amazon, Etsy, or eBay
Pastrymade	Current	www.pastrymade.com
Salvatore's Studio	Current	www.salvatoresstudio.com
The Springerle Baker	Current	www.thespringerlebaker.com
Wilton	Vintage	Try Etsy or eBay
Zanda Panda	Vintage	Try Etsy or eBay

Other Essential Tools

Kitchen knife. For cutting blocks of clay.

Cutting board. I like to use plastic ones in different sizes.

Soft brush. For applying and removing cornstarch. A pastry brush or 1-inch paintbrush works well.

Rolling pin.

Craft knife. Replace the blade often, because a dull blade will drag in your clay.

Small, sharp scissors. Embroidery or manicure scissors work well.

Larger utility scissors.

Cookie sheet or tile.

Oven. Make sure the temperature control is accurate.

Timer.

Rack. For drying or cooling clay items.

Paintbrushes. I've used everything from 1-inch house painter brushes to 20/0 artist brushes. It's worth getting good ones.

Optional Tools

Cutting and Drilling

Wavy edge pastry wheel or straight edge crinkle cutter.

Small saw and miter box. For moldings, used when building freestanding boxes.

Single edge razor blade. Used for making very thin slices.

Pin vise. For drilling small holes.

Polymer clay tool kits often include a *tissue blade.* I've tried several versions of this tool and consider it dangerous. Of course, that's a matter of opinion, but I prefer to use ordinary knives for slicing clay.

Rolling

Rolling pin thickness guides. Useful when you want a uniform thickness.

Dowel or small clay roller. Use small rollers only for initial rolling of small amounts of clay. Don't use rollers to push clay into molds—you're likely to get double or triple images if you do.

Pasta machine. Not necessary, but a big help with conditioning harder clays or larger amounts. Clay artists have told me that the "pasta machines" sold under the same brands as the clay are inferior to those marketed for kitchen use.

Gluing

Hot glue gun. Hot glue can sometimes be used to hold pieces together while your more permanent glue is setting. See my Basic Directions chapter for instructions for "tack gluing."

Sanding

Dremel tool. Can be very useful, though you can easily do without one.

Electric sander. For some of the wood items.

Miscellaneous

I'll grab anything that looks like it might be useful. Here are a few examples.

Cotton swabs. Moistened, they can be used as paint erasers.

Eye shadow applicators. For drybrush painting.

Bamboo skewers. Too many uses to list!

Wig pins. T-shaped pins used for temporary gluing alignment.

Popsicle sticks.

Tweezers.

Bow maker. For if you're not buying pre-made bows for your wreaths and aren't skilled at making them freehand.

Over-the head magnifier. I got one of these when I was bringing my work so close, I was in danger of painting my nose.

Basic Supplies

Now let's look at the supplies you'll need for many or all of my projects. Special supplies needed for individual projects will be listed with those.

Polymer Clay

Two types of polymer clay are used in this book: air-dry clay and bake clay. Within those two main types, you can find a bewildering array of specialties—but for the most part, I've stuck to the basics.

Air-dry clay hardens by itself to a leathery, rubbery, or papery texture. When dry, the pieces aren't particularly fragile. They can be trimmed with scissors or a craft knife, painted, and even sewn to other objects.

Bake clay is baked in an oven to a texture that's somewhat like bisque ceramic. Especially if the piece is thin, it's brittle. It can be sanded and carved after baking.

We'll use different types for different projects, though sometimes either will work. For bake clay, I'll often recommend the "lightweight" variety, since that helps with items that must be supported or hung.

Leftover air-dry clay and lightweight bake clay should be wrapped tightly with plastic wrap and used as soon as possible. Ordinary bake clay supposedly won't react with air but instead remain workable indefinitely. But if that clay is mixed with cornstarch—as clay that you've handled probably will be—you may not have that much time before it becomes flaky. So, wrap this too in plastic wrap to keep it usable.

Polymer clay can be pricey when bought in small amounts. To save money, try searching for it in "bulk" or "wholesale."

Other Essential Supplies

Baking parchment.

Cornstarch. Keeps clay from sticking to the molds. Talcum powder also works.

Sandpaper. Used for projects that include wood pieces, as well as for smoothing baked or dried clay.

Thin cardboard. Used for supporting unmolded clay items before baking or drying.

Wood filler, acrylic modeling paste, or acrylic impasto. All three will fill cracks. Wood filler is grainier, but it will do for most uses. I don't see much difference between acrylic modeling paste and acrylic impasto. Both can be used for fine work or to simulate snow.

Acrylic paints. I mostly recommend "folk art" type bottle paints or other liquid paint. If you use tube paints, thin them with water or acrylic paint thinner. I use straight tube paint for erasing mistakes. For very fine lines, I use acrylic paint pens.

Glues. I mostly use white glue or wood glue. Also epoxy, hot melt, and E6000 jewelry glue. I'll generally specify in the individual project description what I used, and I also recommend checking the glue manufacturer's info to be sure it works on what you're gluing.

Optional Supplies

Sealer. If you want to seal your work, use a product recommended by the clay manufacturer. Some other sealers remain sticky over clay.

Glaze. Polymer clay glazes are compatible with the clay, so they dry without any residue.

Aluminum foil. For propping air-dry clay in the position you want it to dry in.

Paper. For making patterns.

A WORD ABOUT BASKETS

Baskets and polymer clay decorations seem made to go together, and you'll find a number of baskets among my projects.

Any basket can be trimmed with decorations. If the basket is a fine one, and you don't want to glue things directly to it, it's very easy to use the basket weave to support ties. No damage to the basket, and you can remove the decorations at any time. Such temporary decorations also lend themselves to seasonal changes.

Sometimes you can find beautiful baskets that have a little wear or damage—which means they're inexpensive compared to perfect ones. And of course, your decorations can cover the damage.

Basic Directions

This is where you'll learn how to do nearly everything you need to. A few projects will require more, and for those, you'll find special directions with the projects.

Choosing Your Clay

Each project lists a suggested type of clay. To make your own choice, consider the piece's use.

• If the piece is to be hung or mounted on something else—like a basket, box, or Christmas tree—use air-dry clay or lightweight bake clay to reduce weight.

• If the shape needs to be changed or manipulated once the piece leaves the mold—say, to bend or curve it—use air-dry clay.

• If the piece is very thin, use air-dry clay. Some molds have a paper-thin image, and bake clay would be much too brittle at that thickness.

Conditioning Your Clay

Though most air-dry clay and lightweight bake clay is workable right out of the package, ordinary bake clay is another story. Some of it is hard as rocks when you unwrap it. Warming the clay does little or nothing to make it more flexible, so you need to "condition" it. Conditioning may also help air-dry clay or lightweight bake clay when it has partially dried before you've had a chance to use it.

If you have a pasta machine, slice the clay to a thickness of about a quarter inch and run it through the machine at the widest open setting. Fold the clay and repeat a few times. No need to use the thinner settings for most projects. The clay is ready to use when it doesn't break or crumble when you fold it.

If you don't have a pasta machine, cut a very thin slice from the clay and knead it in your hands till it's flexible. Do the same with another slice, then combine and knead the two together. Keep this up till your ball has enough clay for your purpose.

Molding Air-Dry Clay

Here are instructions for molding your air-dry clay. For especially thin pieces, be sure to see the note at the end.

1. If the clay has hardened too much to mold easily, try softening it by conditioning it, following the directions above.

2. Roll the clay to the desired thickness. This will depend on your mold, but a typical range of thickness is an eighth to a quarter inch.

POLYMER CLAY SAFETY

Though polymer clay is classed as nontoxic and meets the Consumer Product Safety Commission's regulations for children's toys, clay manufacturers recommend that the same tools not be used for both polymer clay and food.

Follow the clay manufacturer's directions for baking, and use good ventilation. Avoid overcooking or burning bake clay. To help prevent this, make sure your oven thermostat is accurate, and use a timer.

Polymer clay will sand much faster than wood. If you sand with an electric tool, such as a Dremel tool, wear goggles and a mask, and do it outdoors or at least with good ventilation. This is especially important if you're dry-sanding.

Some people report allergic reactions to polymer clay. If you develop symptoms that might have been caused by the clay, consult your doctor.

3. Cut a piece out of the rolled sheet, a little larger than the mold.

4. With a dry, soft brush, dust both sides of the clay with cornstarch.

5. Push the clay firmly into the mold with your fingers, not with a rolling pin. With the mold on the bottom and the clay on top, press directly on the clay—always straight down, not at an angle, which could give you multiple impressions. If there are hollows in the back side of the clay, fill them in with other bits of clay to flatten the surface. Don't trim off excess around the edges yet—it will help with unmolding.

6. Lay a piece of baking parchment over the clay. You now have a "sandwich" of parchment, clay, and mold. Holding the sandwich together, turn it over so the parchment is at the bottom.

7. Hold down the clay and parchment together while you lift the mold off the clay. (This is where the excess clay around the edges comes in handy.) If the clay doesn't separate easily, go round and round the edges, teasing the clay away from the mold.

8. With a craft knife or cookie cutter, trim excess clay from the edges, then brush off remaining cornstarch.

9. Slide the clay piece with parchment onto a rack. Set it all in a dry, warm place and wait for the clay to harden.

10. Fix flaws as needed, using the directions below.

Note: Air-dry clay can be used to make paper-thin pieces. If that's what you're doing, press in the clay in as thin a layer as you can, then let the piece dry right in the mold, instead of unmolding it as directed above. When dry, an ultra-thin piece will pop out of the mold on its own. You can then trim it with small, sharp scissors.

Molding Bake Clay in a Non-Bakeable Mold

These are instructions for molding your bake clay when the mold itself can't be baked. For especially large pieces, be sure to see the note at the end.

1. If the clay has hardened too much to mold easily, try softening it by conditioning it, following the directions above.

2. Roll the clay to the desired thickness. This will depend on your mold, but a typical range of thickness is an eighth to a quarter inch. If you roll the clay much thinner than one-eighth inch, the clay is likely to tear as you unmold it.

3. Cut a piece out of the rolled sheet, a little larger than the mold.

4. With a dry, soft brush, dust both sides of the clay with cornstarch.

5. Push the clay firmly into the mold with your fingers, not with a rolling pin. With the mold on the bottom and the clay on top, press directly on the clay—always straight down, not at an angle, which could give you multiple impressions. If there are hollows in the back side of the clay, fill them in with other bits of clay to flatten the surface. Don't trim off excess around the edges yet—it will help with unmolding.

6. Lay a piece of baking parchment over the clay. You now have a "sandwich" of parchment, clay, and mold. Holding the sandwich together, turn it over so the parchment is at the bottom.

7. Hold down the clay and parchment together while you lift the mold off the clay. (This is where the excess clay around the edges comes in handy.) If the clay doesn't separate easily, go round and round the edges, teasing the clay away from the mold.

8. With a craft knife or cookie cutter, trim excess clay from the edges, then brush off remaining cornstarch.

9. Slide the clay piece with the parchment onto a cookie sheet. Bake the piece, following the clay manufacturer's instructions. Let it cool before handling.

10. Fix flaws as needed, using the directions below.

Note: If the clay piece is larger than your hand, you can add cardboard over the parchment to help with unmolding. Once you've turned over the "sandwich," you can slide out the cardboard from underneath, or you can keep it there longer to help keep the clay from distorting when you separate it from the mold.

Molding Bake Clay in a Bakeable Mold

Here are instructions for molding your bake clay when the mold too can go in the oven.

1. If the clay has hardened too much to mold easily, try softening it by conditioning it, following the directions above.

2. Roll the clay to the desired thickness. This will depend on your mold, but a typical range of thickness is an eighth to a quarter inch. If you roll the clay much thinner than one-eighth inch, the clay is likely to tear as you unmold it.

3. Cut a piece out of the rolled sheet, a little larger than the mold.

4. With a dry, soft brush, dust both sides of the clay with cornstarch.

5. Push the clay firmly into the mold with your fingers, not with a rolling pin. With the mold on the bottom and the clay on top, press directly on the clay—always straight down, not at an angle, which could give you multiple impressions. If there are hollows in the back side of the clay, fill them in with other bits of clay to flatten the surface.

6. With a craft knife, trim excess clay from the edges.

7. Bake the piece in the mold, following the clay manufacturer's instructions, then put the mold on a rack to cool.

8. After cooling—not before!—remove the piece from the mold and brush off remaining cornstarch.

9. Fix flaws as needed, using the directions below.

Note: In a very few cases, instead of pressing the clay into the mold, you'll need to press the mold down onto the clay. I'll point out when a project requires this and give tips for getting a good impression.

Shaping Air-Dry Clay with a Cookie Cutter

1. If needed, soften the clay by conditioning it, following the directions above.

2. Set a flattened ball of clay on a piece of baking parchment that's slightly larger than the cookie cutter.

3. Roll the clay to the desired thickness.

4. Position the cookie cutter and press down to cut out the shape, then remove the excess clay.

6. Transfer the clay with parchment paper to a rack and let dry.

7. Fix flaws as needed, using the directions below.

Shaping Bake Clay with a Cookie Cutter

1. If needed, soften the clay by conditioning it, following the directions above.

2. Set a flattened ball of clay on a piece of baking parchment that's slightly larger than the cookie cutter.

3. Roll the clay to the desired thickness.

4. Position the cookie cutter and press down to cut out the shape, then remove the excess clay.

6. Transfer the clay with parchment paper to a cookie sheet and bake according to the clay manufacturer's instructions, then let cool before handling.

7. Fix flaws as needed, using the directions below.

Molding a Single Image with a Rolling Pin

1. Roll the clay with an ordinary rolling pin, using guides to get a uniform thickness.

2. Cut a piece out of the rolled sheet, a little larger than the image you want.

3. With a dry, soft brush, dust both sides of the clay with cornstarch.

4. Push the clay firmly onto the rolling pin with your fingers.

5. Carefully peel off the clay piece.

6. With a craft knife or cookie cutter, trim excess clay from the edges, then brush off remaining cornstarch.

7. Dry or bake.

8. Fix flaws as needed, using the directions below.

Rolling pin cookie molds for single images (left) and continuous sheets (right)

Molding a Continuous Sheet with a Rolling Pin

1. On a sheet of parchment, roll out the clay with an ordinary rolling pin, using guides to get a uniform thickness. It's a good idea to make the sheet considerably larger than you'll need in the end, as the quality of your impression may be uneven. This way, you can keep the best area and discard the rest.

2. With a dry, soft brush, dust the top of the clay with cornstarch.

3. Roll your embossed pin very slowly over the clay surface, firmly pressing straight down over the entire sheet. Your work surface must be low enough to allow this. (A kitchen counter is likely too high.)

If the rolling pin is long, you may have to exert extra pressure along its length. Roll the pin a quarter turn at a time, then keep it still as you inch both hands from the ends toward the center, pressing down firmly and evenly at points along the way.

4. With a craft knife, cut your piece to size, then brush off remaining cornstarch.

5. Dry or bake.

6. Fix flaws as needed, using the directions below.

Fixing Flaws

After your clay piece is dried or baked, you may find surface cracks or dents. You don't have to do everything over! For small cracks or rough areas, just rub white glue into them.

You can rebuild larger areas with wood filler, acrylic modeling paste, or acrylic impasto. *Modeling paste* and *impasto* are materials that artists use for texture in painting. They're very similar to each other, but the impasto is more translucent and may dry a little faster. Both are more fine-textured than the wood filler.

Let everything dry thoroughly before proceeding.

Gluing

Check the glue packaging to make sure your glue will work with your clay or whatever else you're gluing. You won't find polymer clay listed as such, but it would come under the heading "porous materials."

Whenever possible—and it isn't always—glue your pieces *before* finishing the surfaces to be glued. Glue holds better on bare polymer clay than on clay coated with paint, sealer, glaze, or any other finish.

Always make sure your gluing is done on a work surface your glue won't adhere to. Glue quite often sneaks into unexpected places, and you do not want newspaper stuck to the back of your project.

Always let glue dry thoroughly before proceeding.

Most glued pieces need to be held together while the glue sets. But for our projects, ordinary clamps are unlikely to work. Luckily, there are several alternatives.

Clamping with clothespins. Ordinary clothespins are useful for some glue jobs. You could also think about binder clips, quilters' clips, fabric clamps, or any other such small clamping devices.

Weighted clamping. Fill one or two zip top plastic sandwich bags with raw rice or beans—or with pie weights, pebbles, or anything heavy. Then use the bags as weights to keep your glue pieces together.

Tack gluing. Toward the edges of the piece, use whatever glue you want—epoxy, white glue, wood glue—but in the center, add a small blob of hot melt glue (from a glue gun) or super glue. Neither of those glues can be counted on for a permanent bond by themselves, but they'll hold the pieces together while the other glue sets.

Sometimes there's not enough surface area between two objects to give a secure glue bond—for example, when attaching a tie cord to the back of a clay medallion. In that particular case, you can use what I call *felted gluing.* Cut a piece of felt sheet roughly in the shape of your medallion, but at least a sixteenth inch smaller all around. Glue the cord across the medallion, then glue the felt over it to sandwich it in. This prevents the cord from popping off the medallion when the piece is in use.

Sample of felted gluing

Painting, Sealing, and Glazing

Some of the painting on my projects may look intricate, but don't let that scare you off. You're not working from a blank sheet—you're applying paint to designs that are already in the molded clay. It's similar to painting in a coloring book, but possibly even easier, because you have the advantage of a raised pattern.

If you're painting a molding of something from real life—say, an animal or plant, instead of an abstract design—it helps to find one or more good photographs of it. That way, you'll get a natural look, with the right colors in the right places. I'm not suggesting you copy anything, just paint as accurately as you can.

I've mostly used acrylic paint for all the projects. Liquid "folk art" type paint is the easiest to use. The consistency is good, and the premixed colors make touch-up a snap. Large sets of these paints with good color variety are inexpensive and easy to find, and most art stores will also stock individual bottles in many shades.

Liquid paints aren't especially opaque. Sometimes this matters, so I do use some tube paints as well. And I use white tube paint to "erase" colors I want to change. Otherwise, a big change like red over green would take as many as four coats of liquid paint.

For fine, thin lines, use an acrylic paint pen. They're available in different widths and colors. Note that pens you fill yourself are for ink, not paint. Some are said to work with thinned paint too, but I haven't had good results from that.

Drybrush painting is a technique that's useful for designs in relief and certainly for cookie mold projects. There are special brushes for this, but I use eye shadow applicators—those short plastic sticks with a sponge at each end. To drybrush a molded surface, first dip a brush or other applicator in the paint, then blot it on paper so most of the paint is gone. Holding the applicator horizontally, dab or rub the tip over only the raised areas on the molding. It takes a little practice, but you can get beautiful effects and often save a lot of time. (See the Majolica Box detail on the next page.)

If the project is one with a finished back, like a Christmas tree ornament, paint the back before you paint the front, to avoid having to repaint edges.

As I said before, don't paint surfaces that will be glued, if you can avoid it. Glue does not adhere well to paint.

Let each color dry before painting another color next to it. And let all the paint dry before doing anything else to the piece.

Sealing is optional. It's very desirable on pieces with intricate painting because it makes it much easier to make changes or correct errors. Glazing too is optional, but it does a lot to brighten and deepen a painted surface.

Many clear coatings don't harden completely over polymer clay but instead remain slightly sticky. So, if you can, stick with a sealer or glaze produced by the manufacturer of your clay, or else find that manufacturer's recommendations. You can also search for suggestions from other users of that clay.

After getting good paintbrushes in the first place, you should also take good care of them. It's worth it in terms of both effort and results. A well-kept inexpensive brush will work better than an expensive one that's choked with old, dried paint. For cleaning brushes, I use ordinary dish soap rather than special brush cleaning soap. It works better, and it's a lot less expensive.

Detail of Majolica Box (page 35)

Part 2
Projects

Halloween Basket Tie-On
Experience Level: Beginning

It's fun and festive to have a special decorated basket for the candies that await your trick-or-treaters. And it's convenient to be able to remove the decoration and use the basket in other ways for the rest of the year.

This project could hardly be easier. Just mold a pumpkin, paint it, and hang it on your chosen basket. Instead of a pumpkin, there are many other Halloween cookie molds you could choose—witches, scarecrows, cats, ghosts—just about anything you might fancy. Just make sure you know whether your mold is bakeable or not!

Clay
Lightweight bake clay

Molds and Cutters
Halloween mold, by Boston Warehouse

Special Tools and Supplies
Wire basket
Ribbon or cord ties

1. Follow my basic directions for molding bake clay in a bakeable mold.

2. Glue the center of a 12-inch cord or ribbon to the top center back of the pumpkin with epoxy glue.

Back view of pumpkin, showing glued cord

3. Paint the pumpkin. If you paint its back, do that first.

4. Seal the front of the pumpkin with polymer clay glaze or gloss sealer.

5. Tie the medallion to the basket.

Square Canister Basket
Experience Level: Beginning

For this project, I wanted to avoid gluing the medallion directly to the basket, but I also wanted a more durable connection than I could get just by gluing a tie cord to clay. So, I came up with the idea of sandwiching a cord between the medallion and a piece of felt sheet, with all of it glued together. This makes sure the cord will never pop away from the medallion. I used thin felt, but you could use a sheet of any thickness. Just choose a color that's not conspicuous.

Of course, you can instead glue the medallion directly to the basket, if you prefer.

Clay
Lightweight bake clay

Molds and Cutters
Bird on Branch with Berries cookie
    mold, by D.D. Dillon
3-inch round scalloped cookie cutter

Special Tools and Supplies
Square canister basket
Thin felt sheet
Thin cord, ribbon, or fishing line

1. Follow my basic directions for molding bake clay in a non-bakeable mold, using the round scalloped cookie cutter to cut out the shape.

2. Paint and glaze the medallion.

3. If you want to glue the medallion to the basket, do that now, and you're done. Otherwise, cut a section of thin cord, ribbon, or fishing line, about two feet long, to use as a tie, and a felt circle slightly smaller than the medallion.

4. Following my basic directions for felted gluing, fasten the center of the tie to the center back of the medallion near the top.

5. When the glue is dry, thread each end of the tie through the basket weave. (With thin cord, you can use a heavy needle for this.) Knot the tie ends together inside the basket. If you're using a decorative ribbon or cord, you can instead cross the ends, bring them back through the weave, and tie them in a bow above the medallion.

Key Basket
Experience Level: Intermediate

Who doesn't need a handy place for keys? Depending on their shape, key baskets can hang on the wall or from a doorknob. Once you get in the habit of using a key basket, you will never lose your keys again.

In this project, several figures were attached independently to a small basket. The large lock was tied with a cord that's sandwiched between the figure and felt backing. The felt keeps the cord from popping off the back of the figure. (I tried clear fishing line instead of cord but found it too shiny to be invisible.)

Clay
Lightweight bake clay

Molds and Cutters
Heart Lock Silicone Cookie Mold, by
    Artesão Cookie Molds
Key fondant molds

Special Tools and Supplies
Small basket
Thin felt sheet
Thin cord or heavy thread

1. For the heart lock, follow my basic directions for molding bake clay in a bakeable mold.

2. For the key, follow my basic directions for molding bake clay in a non-bakeable mold.

3. Paint and glaze the figures.

4. If you want to glue the figures directly to the basket, do that now, and you're done. Otherwise, sew the keys to the basket with thread that matches the color of the key.

5. Cut a section of thin cord or heavy thread about 12 inches long to use as a tie, and a felt disk slightly smaller than the lock.

6. Following my basic directions for felted gluing, fasten the cord and felt backing to the lock.

7. When the glue is dry, thread one end of the tie through a heavy needle and sew it through the basket. Repeat with the other end. Knot the tie ends together inside the basket and cut them near the knot.

• BASKETS •

Picnic Basket

Experience Level: Advanced

Here's a summery basket to take with you on excursions. It's a "collage" basket, with the three molded squares and other pieces glued to each other in layers before being tied to the basket itself. Some brands of baking parchment have a grid on the back, ideal for laying out a geometric design like this.

Though you can't see them in the photos, the top and bottom points of the molded squares are supported by baked clay triangles glued on behind.

Clay
Lightweight bake clay

Molds and Cutters
Flowers and Fruit Shortbread
    Mold, by Brown Bag
    Cookie Art
2-inch square scalloped cookie
    cutter
1-inch square scalloped cookie
    cutter

Special Tools and Supplies
Large basket
Gridded paper or baking
    parchment
Thin felt sheet
Thin cord

Make the Pieces

1. For the three molded squares, follow my basic directions for molding bake clay in a non-bakeable mold, using the three images in the center column of this shortbread pan. Mold the pieces one at a time and trim each with the 2-inch scalloped cookie cutter. (The shortbread pan is actually bakeable, but unmolding before baking allows the edge detailing.)

2. For the other pieces, follow my basic directions for shaping bake clay with a cookie cutter, using the 1-inch scalloped cookie cutter. First cut seven squares, then leaving four as they are, cut the remaining three in half diagonally with a craft knife to make six triangles. (In the finished basket, the triangles will not show from the front.)

3. After baking all pieces, paint and seal the front of each. (I used white for the hidden triangles.)

Assemble the Collage

1. Lay the three molded squares side by side and face down on a piece of gridded paper or baking parchment. Each square should be rotated 45 degrees to present a diamond shape, and their points should be touching.

2. Glue the four plain squares, face down and rotated 45 degrees, to overlap the molded squares at their side corners. (See the photos.)

3. On the top and bottom corners of each molded square, glue one of the six triangles face up.

4. Cut four pieces of thin cord or heavy thread about twelve inches long and glue each one vertically to the center back of one of the plain squares. Cut four felt disks slightly smaller than the squares and glue each one over a cord.

Attach the Collage

1. When the glue is dry, thread one end of a tie through a heavy needle and sew it through the basket. Repeat with the other end. Knot the ends together on the inside of the basket and cut them near the knot.

2. Do the same for the other ties.

• BASKETS •

Sewing Basket
Experience Level: Advanced

The decoration on this basket is a collage of sewing materials and notions, molded and unmolded. Since the pieces could be arranged so many ways, I waited till they were all baked, then played around with them before settling on a final design.

The pincushion mold/cutter is a two-piece set that makes a traditional tomato pincushion with a small attached "strawberry" on a stem. (In a real pincushion of this type, the strawberry would be filled with emery powder and used to hold and sharpen needles.)

A novel feature of this design is that the spool is threaded with real thread, and the pins and needle are also real.

The basket was an old one with some damage on the side, now nicely covered by the decorations.

Make the Pincushion

1. To make the "tomato," roll clay to a thickness of about three-quarters inch and press the pincushion cutter into the clay to mark it. Don't try to cut all the way through—that would make the veins too deep—but instead remove the cutter and finish with a craft knife.

2. Carve the top of the block to make the rounded shape of the pincushion. You'll have half a tomato—rounded on top, with a flat back. Get the top as smooth as you can. (If you need to, you can sand it smoother after baking.)

3. To make the "strawberry" needle holder plus the tomato top, roll clay to a thickness of about one-eighth inch, then use the smaller cutter to cut out the shape.

4. Following my basic instructions for molding bake clay in a non-bakeable mold, bake and cool the pieces. Then glue the strawberry piece to the tomato with epoxy.

Clay
Lightweight bake clay

Molds and Cutters
Quilted wreath mold, by
    Cotton Press
Scissors mold, by Laxa Family
Two-piece pincushion,
    combined mold and cutter,
    by Kato Baking Supplies
Thimble chocolate mold
Spool chocolate mold

Special Tools and Supplies
Large basket
Large embroidery needle
Heavy-duty white thread
Light cord
Ball-headed quilting pins
Fine-point pencil or marker
    with disappearing ink
Wavy edge pastry wheel or
    straight edge crinkle cutter

>

Make the Other Pieces

1. For the scissors and spool, follow my basic directions for molding bake clay in a non-bakeable mold.

2. For the thimble, follow my basic directions for molding bake clay in a non-bakeable mold. Before pressing in the clay, line the mold with plastic wrap, then use that to pull out the clay. Before baking, trim the clay to make a flat side, giving you about three-quarters of a thimble.

3. For the quilt block, follow my basic directions for molding bake clay in a non-bakeable mold. Before baking, use a wavy edge pastry wheel or straight edge crinkle cutter to trim the clay, simulating a pinked edge. (The quilt block mold is actually bakeable, but unmolding before baking allows the edge detailing.)

Assemble the Collage

1. When all pieces are baked and cooled and their flaws fixed, arrange them as you'll want them in the finished work. With a fine-point pencil or a marker with disappearing ink, mark the quilt block where the other pieces rest on it. (This is to make sure you don't paint the quilt block where you'll be gluing pieces.)

2. Paint and glaze the front of all pieces *except* the marked parts of the quilt block and the barrel of the spool.

3. When the paint on the spool is dry, rub white glue or wood glue over the barrel and wind thread around it. Glue both ends of the thread securely to the back of the piece.

4. Following my basic directions for tack gluing, glue the scissors, pincushion, thimble, and spool to the quilt block with epoxy.

5. Thread the embroidery needle and knot the thread. Rub the entire length of the thread with white glue to make it easier to shape, and while the glue is still wet, arrange the thread on the quilt block in a natural curve. Glue the needle too on the quilt block, positioning the needle point so it won't be a hazard to fingers.

Attach the Collage

1. Cut 24-inch lengths of the light cord. You'll need one length for each corner of the quilt block, plus one for each clay piece extending much beyond the block's edges. With epoxy, glue the center of each length of cord to a point that needs attaching.

2. When the glue is cured, thread the ends of each cord through the basket weave, tie the ends securely, and cut them off close to the basket.

3. Stick a few ball-headed pins into the pincushion.

Tissue Box
Experience Level: Beginning

For this project, I chose a cookie mold with four floral shapes and painted them to show each one in a different phase of opening—from closed, to budding, to nearly open, to fully open. They're in a circle, like the seasons.

For subtle shading on the edges of the medallion, either scrape powder from a pastel chalk stick with sandpaper or an emery board, or use pastel chalk in pre-powdered form. Use a soft brush to apply a little chalk before baking, or rub it in with your fingers afterwards.

Clay
Lightweight bake clay

Molds and Cutters
Carved Wood Gingerbread Mold, by DecoLazer

Special Tools and Supplies
Ceramic tissue box
Pastel chalk stick (optional)
Emery board (optional, for powdering chalk)

1. Follow my basic directions for molding bake clay in a non-bakeable mold.

2. (Optional) Apply pastel chalk powder into the clay before or after baking.

3. Paint and seal the front of the medallion.

4. Glue the medallion to the box, following my basic directions for weighted clamping.

Game Box
Experience Level: Intermediate

The box I made for this project is for chessmen, but of course you could make something special for any game. Or make a card box for decks of cards.

I used a marble effect for the chessmen because the box was so plain. It's surprisingly easy to get streaky effects like marble with polymer clay by kneading two colors together. I did it one piece at a time—probably the easiest way.

You could also just paint the chessmen. Color possibilities would be plain black and white, or light and dark wood grain, or gold and silver. But getting a good appearance is easier with the streaky patterns of marble or wood grain than with the shiny look of gold or silver, which makes every bump or irregularity glaringly obvious.

Clay
Lightweight bake clay

Molds and Cutters
Chess Set Springerle Mold and Cutter, by Kitchen Vixen

Special Tools and Supplies
Unfinished wood box with sliding top

1. Sand and finish the box as desired, then mark the spacing for the chessmen.

2. For each chess piece, knead walnut-sized lumps of black and white clay together, either mostly black or mostly white for the different color pieces. Mix only till the clay is streaked and marbled.

3. Follow my basic directions for molding bake clay in a non-bakeable mold.

4. Glue the chessmen to the box with epoxy glue, following my basic directions for weighted clamping.

Round Canister
Experience Level: Intermediate

In this project, you apply a square medallion to a curved surface. Pat the medallion very gently into place when you set it on the surface—you want it to fit snugly to the curve, but avoid pressing it very much, or you'll ruin the image.

It's best to paint the medallion only after it's glued to the canister, since the curved shape is fragile until it's supported.

Clay
Air-dry clay

Molds and Cutters
Cherries Mold, by House on the Hill
2-inch square cookie cutter

Special Tools and Supplies
Ceramic food storage canister with laminated bamboo top
Padded box or basket
Masking tape or china marker
Blue painter's tape

Prepare the Canister

1. With the canister lid removed, use masking tape, a china marker, or other guide line to mark around the boundaries where the medallion will go.
2. Wrap the canister tightly with plastic wrap. The area for the medallion should be free of any wrinkles or crumples.

3. With the medallion area facing up, pack the canister in a padded box or other "nest" so it can't roll while you work on it. (I used a plastic organizer basket stuffed with packing foam, but a cardboard box and crumpled newspaper would do just as well.)

Make the Square Medallion

1. Follow my basic directions for molding air-dry clay, trimming with the square cookie cutter.

2. With the plastic wrap still on the canister, lay the cut-out medallion in the spot where it will be attached. Gently push it down onto the curved surface, being careful not to damage the design.

3. Put the box with canister in a warm place and let the medallion dry at least overnight.

4. Carefully remove the medallion and set it aside to finish drying.

Attach and Finish the Medallion

1. Remove the plastic wrap from the canister and put it back in its "nest."

2. Glue the medallion to the canister, following my basic directions for tack gluing and using your tape or markings as a guide. Let the glue dry before taking the canister out of the "nest."

3. Fix any flaws in the medallion, then paint and glaze it, protecting the canister as needed with blue painter's tape.

Mermaid Box Set
Experience Level: Intermediate

For this project, I converted a set of three unfinished boxes and a tray into a hair accessories caddy, ornamented with mermaids and other sea figures. The small figures on top are optional, but they do help me remember what's in the boxes—for example, the one with the crab contains claw clips.

Glue the figures to the boxes only with the whole set assembled—including the tray—to make sure everything will fit in place.

Prepare the Boxes and Tray

1. Sand the boxes and tray.

2. Paint the boxes with a mixture of gloss water-base sealer and lime green metallic acrylic paint. (This gives a shiny, transparent effect, with wood grain showing through.)

3. Paint the exterior of the tray with sand paint. (I also used sand paint on two areas of the lids.)

4. Paint the interior of the tray with acrylic paint to match the color of the sand paint.

Make the Figures

1. For the upright mermaid, follow my basic directions for molding bake clay in a non-bakeable mold.

2. For the seated mermaid and the large shell, follow my basic directions for molding bake clay in a bakeable mold.

3. For your other sea figures, follow my basic directions for molding air-dry clay.

4. Paint all figures. (I used iridescent acrylic paint on the mermaid tails, pearl white acrylic paint on the shell exterior, and coral metallic acrylic paint on the shell lining.)

Clay
Lightweight bake clay (for mermaids and large shell)
Air-dry clay (for other sea figures)

Molds and Cutters
Seated mermaid mold, by Salvatore's Studio
Mermaid springerle mold, by Kitchen Vixen
Shell mold, by Cotton Press
Silicone molds for other sea figures

Special Tools and Supplies
Set of three unfinished wood boxes and tray
Sand paint
Metallic acrylic paint, lime green
Metallic acrylic paint, coral (optional)
Iridescent acrylic paint (optional)
Pearl white acrylic paint (optional)
Artificial pearl (optional)

Assemble

1. Glue the figures to the boxes. For the mermaids and the large shell, follow my basic directions for tack gluing. For your other sea life, follow my basic directions for weighted clamping. Make sure to keep all figures away from the bottom edges of the boxes, which will be covered by the tray rim.

2. (Optional) Glue the artificial pearl to a small shell on the lid with a dot of epoxy.

Majolica Box
Experience Level: Advanced

This project starts with an unfinished wood box, available online or in craft stores. The clay is molded with an embossed rolling pin and glued to the box sides.

You can make something like this with any allover-pattern cookie rolling pin. They're available online in dozens of patterns—holiday, paisley, children's designs—almost anything you can think of. Some of these pins are cut rather shallow and require hard pressure to make a good image. Others, especially reproductions of antique rolling pins, are easier to use.

Painting and detailing are intricate but done fairly easily with the drybrush technique. A brief explanation of this is given in my basic directions for painting, and you can find more detailed instructions online.

The clay side pieces are made two at a time for opposite sides of the box. This makes it possible to fit them properly.

I reinforced the underside of the lid with a thin wood piece, but it does complicate construction. If you decide to omit it, you should add a 1-inch washer to the cabinet knob's hardware.

The box edges are trimmed with ornamental wood moldings made for dollhouses. Many styles are available. I used a plain L-shaped molding for the corners, and a rope molding for the bottom edges.

I used a cabochon mold for the feet, but there are many choices. For example, you could shape the clay with a cookie cutter or melon baller. Or you could use wood beads or jewelry box feet.

Clay
Lightweight bake clay

Molds and Cutters
Majolica rolling pin, by DiamondWoodcomua
Cabochon mold (optional, for the box feet)

Special Tools and Supplies
Unfinished wood box (without lid)*
Unfinished wood rectangle, $\frac{1}{16}$ inch thick (for underside of lid)**
$\frac{1}{8}$-inch square wood dowels (for the box lid edges)
Cabinet knob
$\frac{1}{2}$-inch corner dollhouse molding (optional, for box corners)
$\frac{1}{2}$-inch rope dollhouse molding (optional, for box bottom edge)

*My box was 7 x 7 x 4 inches.

**The wood rectangle must be large enough to overhang the box *with* its added clay walls by at least ¼ inch on each side. My rectangle was a nominal 8 inches square, with rounded corners.

Make the Side Pieces

1. Make a paper pattern from one side of the wood box by laying that side down on a sheet of paper and tracing around it. Cut out the pattern, lay it against the box, and trim as needed to get the size exact.

2. Using a plain rolling pin with thickness guides, roll the clay out evenly to an area larger than the paper pattern.

3. With the patterned rolling pin, follow my basic directions for molding a continuous sheet with a rolling pin, getting as sharp an impression as you can. (But don't worry too much if some of it isn't perfect, because you can do a lot with paint and acrylic modeling paste.)

4. Lay the paper pattern on top of the clay. Gently hold it in place and trim the clay around the edges.

5. Repeat steps 2 to 4 for the opposite side of the box.

6. Bake the pieces and cool.

7. Paint and glaze the pieces.

8. Glue the clay pieces to the wood box, following my basic directions for tack gluing.

9. When the glue is dry, repeat the steps above for the other two side pieces. This time, though, your paper pattern will include the added width of the side pieces already attached. That way, the new pieces will overlap the old ones at the corners.

Make the Lid

1. Place the unfinished wood rectangle on a sheet of paper and trace around the perimeter, then trim the pattern to exact size.

2. Roll out the clay, mold it, and trim it as you did with the side pieces.

3. Fold the paper pattern in half and in half again, to find the center of the pattern. Then lay the pattern on top of the unbaked box lid and make a hole through the center to fit the threaded shaft of the cabinet knob.

4. Bake the lid piece and cool.

5. Paint and glaze the top of the lid piece.

6. Glue the lid piece to the unfinished wood rectangle.

7. Using the hole in the clay piece as a guide, drill through the wood rectangle to extend the hole for the cabinet knob.

8. Glue the ⅛-inch square wood dowels to the wood rectangle edges to keep the top from shifting on the box. Make sure they're placed with enough room to fit properly over the box rim! You can check this before gluing by laying the lid upside down with the dowels in place and turning the box over to rest on top. (If there's not enough room to place the dowels at the very edges, you can move them inward so they'll fit *inside* the box.)

9. Paint and seal the underside of the lid.

10. Add the knob.

Top and bottom views of lid. For enlarged view of top, see page 20.

Finish the Box

1. Paint and seal the interior of the box.

2. (Optional) Trim the edges and corners with miniature wood moldings, painting them before gluing them to the box.

3. (Optional) Mold the feet, paint them, and glue them to the box.

Seasonal Candleholder

Experience Level: Beginning

This project calls for a glass candleholder, but you could use a wood or metal one instead, as long as the surface is flat and at least one inch wide and six inches high.

I made the medallions to be interchangeable on a single candleholder, attaching them with a temporary adhesive. You might also attach them permanently, with summer on one side and winter on the other. Or use a pair of candleholders, with one medallion on each.

Clay
Air-dry clay

Molds and Cutters
Flower Staff Ladyfinger springerle mold,
    by Änis-Paradies
Winter Staff Ladyfinger springerle mold,
    by Änis-Paradies

Special Tools and Supplies
Glass candle holder(s) with flat surface
Quake Hold or Museum Wax (optional)

1. Follow my basic directions for molding air-dry clay.

2. Paint the fronts, then seal with gloss sealer, if desired.

3. For a seasonally changeable candleholder, apply a thin film of Quake Hold or Museum Wax to the back of the medallion and press it into place. Otherwise, permanently glue the medallions into place, following my basic directions for weighted clamping.

Keepsake Photo Frame
Experience Level: Beginning

In this project, small square tiles are molded on an embossed rolling pin. I chose a rolling pin with small stylized animals, which I found ideal for this. The same squares could be used to decorate anything for a small child's or baby's room.

Instead of rolling the pin onto the clay, I pressed clay down onto individual images on the rolling pin. I got much clearer images that way.

Clay
Air-dry clay

Molds and Cutters
Animals rolling pin, by Pastrymade
Meadowlands Monogram Springerle Mold, by
    House on the Hill
1½-inch square scalloped cookie cutter

Special Tools and Supplies
Unfinished picture frame

The mold for the letters on top got double duty, because I used the same one for my Alphabet Bookend (page 45).

I chose to buy an unfinished picture frame and finish it myself, but of course, you could buy one already finished.

1. For the animals, follow my basic directions for molding a single image with a rolling pin. Before drying, trim the edges with the square scalloped cookie cutter.

2. For the letters, follow my basic directions for molding air-dry clay. Before drying, trim the edges with a craft knife.

3. Paint and glaze the figures as desired.

4. Finish the picture frame as desired.

5. Arrange all pieces on the frame and glue with epoxy, following my basic directions for weighted clamping.

Baby photo courtesy Unsplash

Valentine Centerpiece
Experience Level: Intermediate

For this project, I constructed a box that had sides and bottom of clay alone. The only wood pieces are the corner braces and trim. (For another example of corner bracing, including an interior photo, see the Gingerbread House project on page 67.)

The front and back pieces were molded in a scalloped round shortbread pan with eight wedge-shaped sections and a heart on each one. Each piece was formed from half of this circle—four wedges, four hearts. Similar shortbread pans are available in many designs—holiday, floral, fruit, animals…many choices. Their shapes may be round, square, or octagonal.

The easiest way to unmold clay from a large mold like this is to do it in pieces, so I molded the halves one at a time.

When the box was done, I filled it with floral foam, letting me use it with either natural or artificial flowers. Of course, you could instead add one or more vases or jars. But I don't recommend filling the box with wet soil or water!

Clay
Bake clay

Molds and Cutters
Valentine Cake Topper mold, by Zanda Panda
3-inch square cookie cutter

Special Tools and Supplies
½-inch square dowel, 8 inches
½-inch dollhouse corner molding, about 18 inches
Floral foam

Make the Box Sides

1. For the front and back pieces, follow my basic directions for molding bake clay in a non-bakeable mold, filling only half of the mold at a time for each piece. Before baking, trim along the pattern's center line with a craft knife.

2. For the two end pieces, follow my basic directions for shaping bake clay with a cookie cutter, using the 3-inch square cookie cutter and then baking.

3. Cut four two-inch lengths of square dowel. On the back of each end piece, center a dowel flush along each vertical edge and glue it in place.

4. Glue the front and back pieces to the vertical dowels on the end pieces. (I chose to inset the end pieces by two scallops from the actual end, but position them as you like.) You will now have a box that's open at top and bottom.

Make the Box Bottom

1. From the bottom of the assembled sides, make a paper pattern for a bottom piece. The pattern should include the area entirely enclosed by the front, back, and end pieces, plus the thickness of the sides themselves.

2. Roll a sheet of clay about one-quarter inch thick and use your pattern to cut it to shape.

3. Bake and cool the bottom piece, then sand the edges if it needs further fitting.

4. Glue the bottom in place.

Finish the Box

1. Paint and seal the box.

2. Cut two pieces of dollhouse corner molding to nearly the length of the front and back pieces. Paint the moldings, then glue them to the bottom edges.

3. Glaze the box and moldings. If you'll be using the box with natural flowers, glaze the interior as well.

4. Fill the box with floral foam and arrange your flowers.

End view of centerpiece, showing inset end piece

Storybook Shelf Standers
Experience Level: Intermediate

Storybook characters make a fun project for a kid's room. The figures are braced by a tab in back that extends down into the base. Without this tab, there wouldn't be enough connection between the base and the figure to hold it permanently.

To glue the tabs in the bases, be sure to use epoxy, which expands as it sets. Most glues shrink, which can let the inserted piece come loose over time.

Of course, you can make shelf standers with many other cookie molds as well. Use them for holiday decorations, kitchen decor, or to brighten a bookcase.

1. For the figures, follow my basic directions for molding bake clay in a bakeable mold. Paint and seal the fronts of the figures, but leave the backs unpainted for now.

2. For the tabs, follow my basic directions for shaping bake clay with a cookie cutter, rolling the clay to about a quarter inch thick and using the 1½-inch square cookie cutter. Before baking, trim each piece to fit behind one of the figures at its bottom.

Clay
Bake clay

Molds and Cutters
Three Bears and Goldilocks
    molds, by Hartstone
    Cookie Molds
3-inch round scalloped cookie
    cutter
1½-inch square cookie cutter

3. For the bases, follow my basic directions for shaping bake clay with a cookie cutter, rolling the clay to about an eighth inch thick and using the round scalloped cookie cutter. Before baking, stand a baked tab on the center of each base and push down to mark the position, then use a craft knife to cut all the way through the base to form a socket for the tab.

4. When the bases are baked, make sure there's a tab that can fit each socket hole. As needed, sand to fit. Then glue the tabs into the holes with epoxy and let it set. For best coverage, place your glue around the top inside rim of the hole, not on the tab. After pushing the tab through, remove excess glue from the bottom.

5. Paint and seal the tops and edges of the bases.

6. Glue a figure to each tab, matching the figure to the tab you've shaped to fit it.

7. When the glue has set, paint the backs of the figures and tabs.

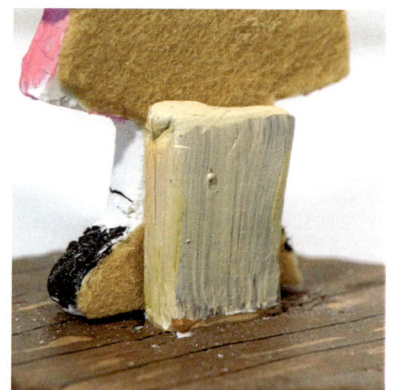

Back view of Goldilocks shelf stander, showing support tab (as well as felt backing that it really didn't need)

Village Planter Box
Experience Level: Advanced

For this project, I made four buildings in the style of the late nineteenth century and lined them up on a finished planter box. The most challenging part was the painting, with fine lines outlining windows and doors.

Like almost any wood planter box, this one would work best for artificial plants, or as a decorative shell for another planter. Another good use would be as a mantel box with candles.

You could decorate it further with miniatures for holidays. Use miniatures at a scale of a quarter inch to a foot, or O-scale railroad figures.

Clay
Lightweight bake clay (for buildings)
Air-dry clay (for trees)

Molds and Cutters
Buildings, by Hartstone Cookie Molds
Christmas tree silicone mold

Special Tools and Supplies
Finished wood box
Ruler or yardstick

Make the Pieces

1. For the buildings, follow my basic directions for molding bake clay in a bakeable mold.

2. Holding each building against the box, mark a line on its back where it meets the box's top edge. Paint the back of the building above this line. (I used matte black paint.)

3. Paint and seal the building fronts. For the window glass, use gray paint highlighted with silver paint. For the fine details around the windows, use 7-millimeter acrylic paint pens. Apply gloss sealer or clear nail polish to the windows, and matte sealer to the rest.

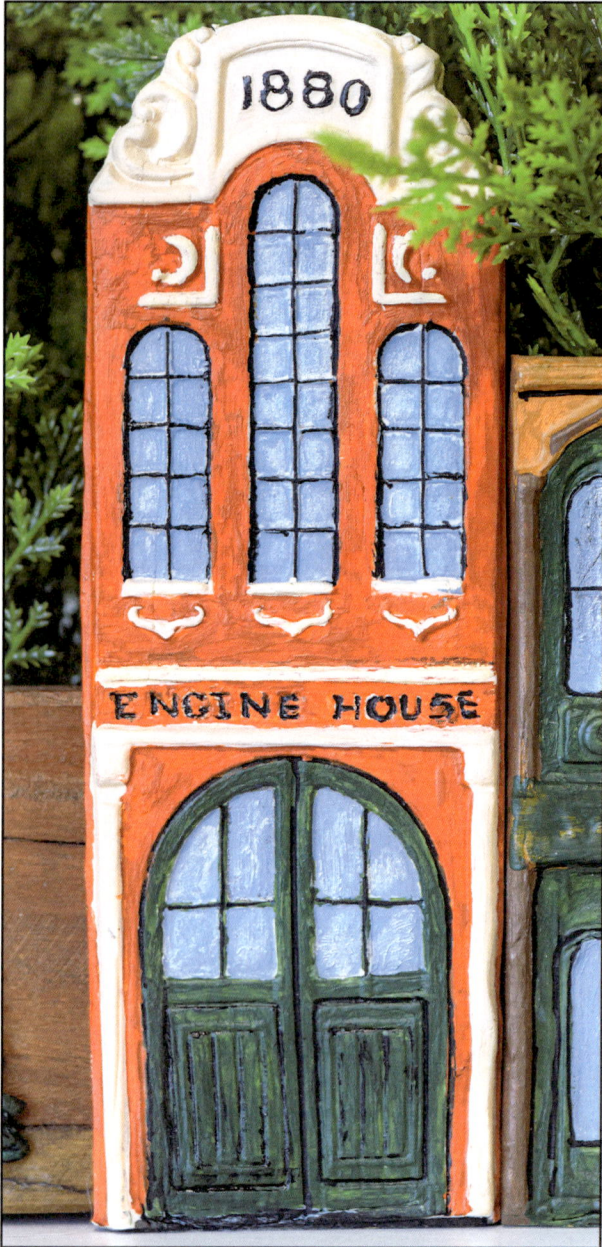

4. For the trees, follow my basic directions for molding air-dry clay, then paint and seal the fronts.

Assemble

1. Line up the buildings in the arrangement you want and measure to find the midpoint of this line. Unless that point falls between two buildings—unlikely, since the buildings are different widths—mark it on the back of the clay piece.

2. Find the midpoint between the ends of the box and mark it.

3. Matching the marked midpoints of the box and the building arrangement, glue the unpainted parts of the buildings to the box, following my basic directions for tack gluing.

4. Also with tack gluing, glue the trees onto the box, to the left and right of the buildings.

Alphabet Bookend
Experience Level: Advanced

The cookie mold for this project is called a hornbook mold, named after alphabet tablets that go back to medieval times. It's not known when such molds first appeared, but the design of the one I chose probably comes from before the sixteenth century. How do I know? Because it omits the letter *J*, the last letter added to the English alphabet!

I used beige clay so I wouldn't have to paint the background. Also, I applied matte sealer to the baked tablet before starting the detailed decorative painting. That made it much easier to correct errors.

The tablet could have been glued directly to the bookend, but instead, I constructed a wood sleeve to glue it to. That way, I can lift off the whole assembly and place it on a different bookend. The wood pieces must be at least as large as the tablet (5½ x 8 inches), but beyond that, they must be wide enough for you to add square dowels at the edges while still fitting the sleeve over the vertical arm of the bookend. (The pieces I used were about 7 x 10½ inches.)

Make sure your bookend is T-shaped, with supporting flanges extending both forward and backward. (An L-shaped bookend might be pulled over by the weight of the tablet.) You also want to make sure the bookend's vertical arm is tall enough to properly support the wood sleeve.

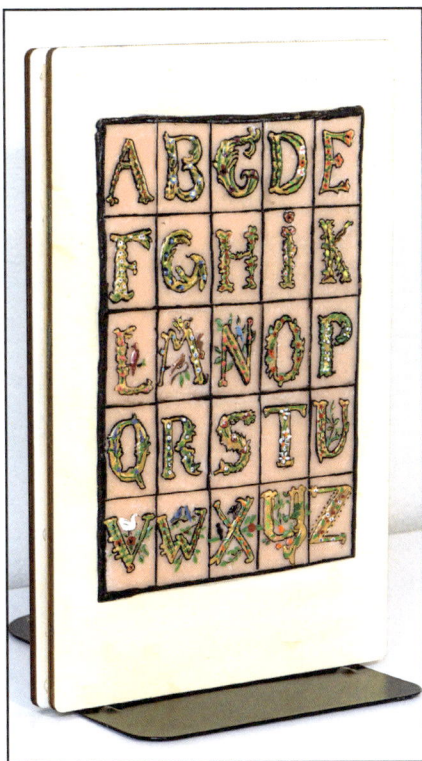

Clay
Lightweight bake clay

Molds and Cutters
Meadowlands Monogram Springerle Mold, by House on the Hill

Special Tools and Supplies
2 unfinished wood pieces, ³⁄₁₆ inch thick, 7 x 10 inches or larger
¼-inch square wood dowel, 20 inches
Metal T-shaped bookend

1. Make the alphabet tablet, following my basic directions for molding bake clay in a non-bakeable mold.

2. Seal the front of the tablet with matte sealer, then paint the letters and borders. Finish with gloss sealer or polymer glaze.

3. Glue the tablet to one of the unfinished wood pieces, following my basic directions for weighted clamping.

4. Cut the wood dowel into two pieces of equal length. Glue them to the back of one wood piece along the vertical edges, using white glue or wood glue and following my basic directions for tack gluing. After the glue dries, attach the other wood piece to the dowels, also with tack gluing.

5. Slip the wood sleeve over the vertical arm of the bookend.

For detail view, see page 8.

Top view of bookend, showing interior construction

Door Signs
Experience Level: Beginning

A cookie mold of a favorite animal or other interest can make you a great decoration for a door sign. The signs I made for this project are designed for kids' rooms, but other molds would work well for a kitchen, workshop, or studio.

The dog and dinosaur molds are pottery, so the medallions are baked in the molds. The unbranded unicorn mold *might* be safe for oven use, but lacking information about it, I treated it as non-bakeable.

Clay
Lightweight bake clay

Molds and Cutters
Dog, by Brown Bag Cookie Art
Dinosaur, by Brown Bag Cookie Art
Unicorn silicone mold

Special Tools and Supplies
3 unfinished wood door signs with cords
Unfinished wood letters

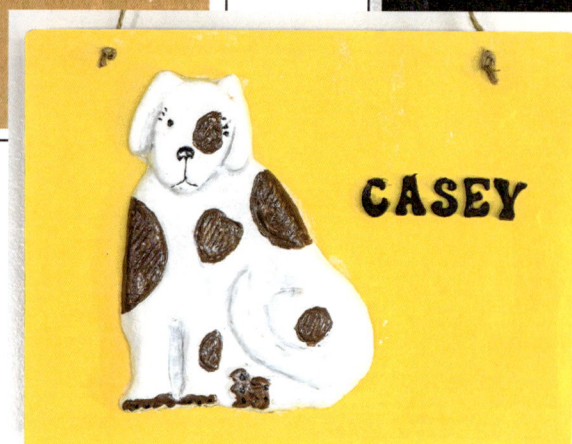

1. For the dog and dinosaur, follow my basic directions for molding bake clay in a bakeable mold. For the unicorn, follow my basic directions for molding bake clay in a non-bakeable mold.

2. Paint and glaze the front of the clay pieces.

3. Glue the clay pieces to the unfinished wood door signs with white glue or wood glue, following my basic directions for tack gluing.

4. Paint and seal the wood signs.

5. Paint and seal the letters for the names on their fronts only, then glue them to the signs with epoxy, following my basic directions for weighted clamping.

6. Add the cords.

Thanksgiving Wreath
Experience Level: Beginning

A door wreath for Thanksgiving is a nice touch for family gatherings. For this one, I added medallions to a ready-made wreath, making it quick and easy.

I used a wreath with pampas grass for its fall color, but eucalyptus or other foliage would also be good. If you prefer to use fresh greens, you can easily remove the medallions to save for the next year.

Don't hang the wreath where it will be exposed to the weather.

Clay
Lightweight bake clay

Molds and Cutters
Peace & Plenty, by Hartstone Cookie Molds
Thankful soap mold, by Morgan's Corner Shop

Special Tools and Supplies
Wreath form with artificial foliage
20-gauge aluminum wire
Thin felt sheet

1. Make the Peace and Plenty medallion, following my basic directions for molding bake clay in a bakeable mold.

2. Make the Thankful medallion, following my basic directions for molding bake clay in a non-bakeable mold.

3. Paint and glaze the medallions.

4. Cut two lengths of wire to make the ties. Each length should be about eight inches longer than the height of its medallion.

5. Center each wire vertically on the back of a medallion, with its ends projecting equally above and below. Glue with epoxy, following my basic directions for tack gluing.

6. Cut a piece of felt sheet to fit the back of each medallion and attach it with white glue or wood glue.

7. When the glue is dry, mount each medallion on the wreath by twisting the wire through and around the wreath structure, then trim the ends of the wire as needed.

8. Make a hanging loop of wire and attach it to the wreath.

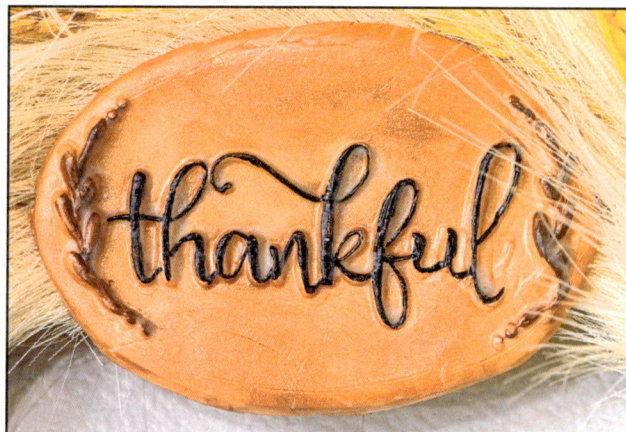

Wedding Wreath
Experience Level: Intermediate

Here's a lovely way to welcome guests for a very special occasion! It could also be a wreath for Valentine's Day.

My directions call for decorating a plain wire wreath form. You can also find forms with pipe cleaners already attached, coming with their own directions.

Don't hang the wreath where it will be exposed to the weather.

Clay
Lightweight bake clay

Molds and Cutters
Quilted Heart mold, by House on the Hill
Valentine springerle mold, by House on the Hill
Heart-shaped cookie cutters (optional)

Special Tools and Supplies
15-inch wire wreath form
10-inch gold mesh ribbon
10-inch white mesh ribbon
1-inch white glitter ribbon
2½-inch wired gold ribbon
White tissue paper
Aluminum wire or fishing line (for the hanging loop)
8-inch white pipe cleaners

Make the Heart Figures

1. Follow my basic directions for molding bake clay in a non-bakeable mold.
2. Paint and glaze the figures.

Cover the Wreath Form

1. Hold the midpoint of a pipe cleaner against the wreath form's outer ring and twist the ends to secure it in place. With both ends now projecting from the wreath front, glue the twisted middle to the wreath form with epoxy. Repeat around the outer ring, spacing the pipe cleaners about four inches apart.
2. Repeat around the innermost ring. These pipe cleaners too should be about four inches apart, but spaced between the ones on the outer ring.
3. Make a hanging loop around the outer ring with aluminum wire or fishing line.
4. Working around the pipe cleaners and hanging loop, tightly wrap white tissue paper around the entire form to conceal the wire. Then wrap 1-inch white glitter ribbon over the tissue to cover that.

Add the Mesh Ribbon

1. Secure one end of the 10-inch white mesh ribbon to the inner ring by twisting the ends of a pipe cleaner around it.

2. Grab the ribbon about nine inches away from the secured point. Bunching up the ribbon in between, position the part you're holding over the next pipe cleaner on the ring and secure the ribbon there too. You'll wind up with nine inches of ribbon in a shortened space of four inches, creating a puff.
3. Continue like that around the inner ring. At the end, cut the ribbon, and then fold it under so the cut doesn't show.
4. Using the 10-inch gold mesh ribbon, repeat these steps on the outer ring.
5. Glue the twisted areas of the pipe cleaners with white glue or wood glue to prevent them coming undone.

Add the Figures and Bows

1. Arrange the loose ends of selected pipe cleaners on the wreath to form beds for gluing the heart figures. Glue each figure to a pipe cleaner bed with epoxy, following my basic directions for tack gluing.
2. Cut off the loose ends of the remaining exposed pipe cleaners.
3. With the 2½-inch wired gold ribbon, make enough bows to cover each of the exposed pipe cleaners, then glue the bows to the twisted areas with white glue or wood glue.
4. (Optional) Make a single larger bow and add it at bottom left or right.

Halloween Wreath
Experience Level: Intermediate

This wreath is so much fun to make! It's easy to make it look eerie and mysterious, and you almost can't do anything wrong.

The moon and cat are supported by wire braces extending from the wreath, rather than being attached to it directly.

Don't hang the wreath where it will be exposed to the weather.

Clay
Lightweight bake clay (for cat, witch, moon, pumpkin)
Air-dry clay (for bats, spider web, owl)

Molds and Cutters
Halloween mold, by Boston Warehouse (for witch)
Scaredy-Cat Mold, by Brown Bag Cookie Art
Sun Moon Stars Celestial Mold, by Brown Bag Paper Art
Pumpkin mold, by Lily of the Valley Clay
Spider web candy mold, by Wilton
Bats silicone mold
Owl candy mold

Special Tools and Supplies
12-inch grapevine wreath form
Artificial manzanita branches
Brown or black floral wire
20-gauge aluminum wire
Halloween ribbon (optional)

Make the Figures

1. For the witch, moon, pumpkin, and cat, follow my basic directions for molding bake clay in a bakeable mold.

2. For the bats, spider web, and owl, follow my basic directions for molding air-dry clay.

3. Paint and glaze the fronts of all pieces, but not the backs.

Make the Wreath

1. Make a hanging loop with 20-gauge aluminum wire, attached to the back of the wreath form.

2. Attach the artificial manzanita branches to the front of the wreath form with floral wire.

3. Make supporting braces from aluminum wire for the cat and moon figures. The wire should form an upside-down U to fit the shape of the figure, with each end extending about six inches below for attaching it. Paint the ends brown or black to match the wreath form, then weave or twine them into the form.

Assemble

1. Glue the witch and cat to their wire braces with epoxy, following my basic directions for tack gluing.

2. Glue the owl, bats, spider web, and pumpkin directly to the wreath, following my basic directions for weighted clamping.

3. (Optional) Make a bow from Halloween ribbon and attach it to the wreath with floral wire.

Back view of cat, showing wire brace

Sunflower Potted Plant Stake
Experience Level: Beginning

At least for me, plants come and go. So this molded sunflower is meant to be removable, attached to the plant stake with a wrapped wire glued only to the figure's back. It's easy to make, and a fun addition to a potted plant, artificial or real.

Clay
Lightweight bake clay

Molds and Cutters
Sunflower, by Artesão Cookie Molds

Special Tools and Supplies
Plant stake
Beading wire
Red or rust powdered pastel chalk
    (optional)

1. Follow my basic directions for molding bake clay in a bakeable mold.

2. (Optional) For cheek color, rub red or rust powdered pastel chalk into the clay after baking.

3. Paint the front of the sunflower and seal with gloss waterproof sealer.

4. Cut about an 18-inch length of beading wire as a tie. Lay it horizontally against the back of the sunflower, with ends extending to each side. Glue it with epoxy, following my basic directions for tack gluing.

5. (Optional) Paint the back of the sunflower and seal with gloss waterproof sealer.

6. Wrap the wire around the plant stake.

Butterfly Floral Picks
Experience Level: Beginning

Butterflies alight on your flowers. This is a very easy project that uses wire to shape the clay. You can paint the butterflies realistically or use fantasy colors. Add them to a floral arrangement of your choice, natural or artificial.

Clay
Air-dry clay

Molds and Cutters
Butterfly cookie mold, by Alfred E Knobler

Special Tools and Supplies
Beading wire
Bamboo skewers, floral wire, or clear canapé skewers
Pin vise
Floral picks (optional)
Floral tape (optional)

1. For each butterfly, cut two four-inch lengths of beading wire.

2. Follow my basic directions for molding air-dry clay, rolling the clay thinly. While the clay is still in the mold, lay the lengths of beading wire diagonally across the butterfly to form an X. Gently press the wire into the clay, and if needed, cover it with small, thin pieces of clay.

3. Before drying, bend the wings of the butterflies to the desired positions.

4. After drying and trimming, paint and seal the butterflies.

5. For each butterfly body, use a pin vise to drill a small vertical hole to fit a bamboo skewer, clear canapé skewer, or floral wire, then glue that in with epoxy.

6. (Optional) If your supports are too short, extend them with floral picks and floral tape.

7. (Optional) If your supports aren't clear, paint them to match the leaves or flowers of your floral arrangement.

Tree of Life Family Album
Experience Level: Intermediate

A large tree of life with many branches and leaves decorates the cover of an album. This would make a beautiful gift.

Clay
Lightweight bake clay

Molds and Cutters
Tree of Life Pie Topper, by My Cookie Mold

Special Tools and Supplies
Photo album
Blue painter's tape

1. Follow my basic directions for molding bake clay in a non-bakeable mold.

2. Paint the medallion, and seal or glaze it.

3. Measuring the album cover, mark out the area for the medallion with blue painter's tape.

4. Spread white glue or wood glue thinly on the back of the medallion, taking care to spread the glue all the way to the edge. Then lay the medallion in the marked area on the album cover and follow my basic directions for weighted clamping.

5. When the glue is dry, remove the tape.

Christmas Tree Ornaments
Experience Level: Beginning

This project is for making figures to hang on your Christmas tree—or anywhere else, for that matter, like on a wall or even a doorknob. Or you could brighten a gift by tying one to the package bow as an *additional* gift.

If you do hang the ornaments on a tree, paint the backs to match the tree color.

Clay
Lightweight bake clay

Molds and Cutters
Angels, by Hartstone Cookie Molds
Rocking Horse mold, by Cotton Press
Eva's Lace mold and cutter, by Kitchen Vixen
Santa mold, by WhysperFairy
Dala Horse mold, by Juno3DStore

Special Tools and Supplies
Ribbon, cord, or fishing line (for hanging)

---

1. Follow my basic directions for molding bake clay in a non-bakeable mold.

2. Cut lengths of ribbon, cord, or fishing line and glue them with epoxy to the back of each figure to form a loop for hanging. Keep in mind how the figure will balance when hung. Some shapes do well with a narrow loop, while others, like the rocking horse, should have a loop with a wide base so the figure stays level.

3. Paint the backs of the figures. To keep the hanging loops out of the way, roll them up like pin curls and fasten them with a clip or bobby pin.

4. Paint and glaze the fronts.

Christmas Candleholder
Experience Level: Beginning

The Christmas tree mold I used for this project is one of my favorite molds all around. The shape is great, and it's also easy to unmold, so I often use it when I teach cookie molding.

To pretty up the tree figure, I used ball ornaments and crystals. You can get many other types of ornaments at a dollhouse scale of one inch to a foot, which is right for this tree.

Clay
Lightweight bake clay

Molds and Cutters
Christmas tree mold, by Wilton

Special Tools and Supplies
Wood candle holder
Miniature Christmas tree ball ornaments
    or beads
Rhinestones

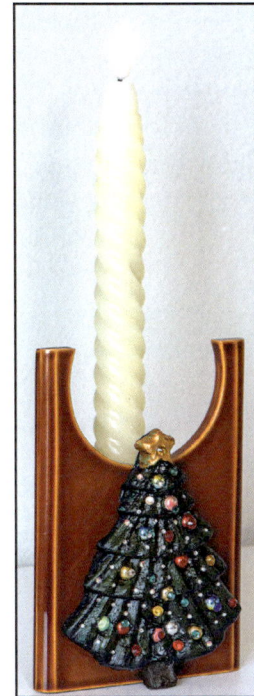

1. Follow my basic directions for molding bake clay in a non-bakeable mold. Before baking, poke holes through the clay for the ball ornaments or beads. These holes should be wide enough for the ornaments to fit inside them and should go all the way through the clay. (The mold is actually bake-able, but unmolding before baking allows making the holes.)

2. Paint and glaze the front of the figure.

3. If the figure will extend past the edges of the candleholder, also finish the parts of the back that will be visible.

4. Glue the ball ornaments and rhinestones in place on the figure with epoxy.

5. Glue the figure to the candleholder.

Saint Nicholas Shelf Stander
Experience Level: Intermediate

Saint Nicholas is, of course, the historical Santa Claus, though this figure's history too is enshrouded in legend. For instance, he is said to have provided dowry money anonymously for daughters of the poor to save them from prostitution.

Today, Saint Nicholas is associated with children's toys as well as with charitable donations. Saint Nicholas Day is December 6, though in some countries, the celebrations take place on the days leading up to that. This is the time when traditional St. Nicholas cookies are made, and for many families, it's the beginning of the Christmas season.

The figure is braced by a tab in back that extends down into the base. For another example of tab bracing, with a photo, see the Storybook Shelf Standers project on page 41.

Recognize the mold? It's featured on the cover and in the instructions of my book *Baking with Cookie Molds*!

For enlarged view, see page 6.

Clay
Bake clay

Molds and Cutters
Saint Nicholas mold, by HOBI Cookie Molds
3-inch round scalloped cookie cutter (for base)
1½-inch square cookie cutter (for tab)

Special Tools and Supplies
Mica powder and glitter (optional, for snow)

1. For the figure, follow my basic directions for molding bake clay in a non-bakeable mold. Paint and seal the front of the figure, but leave the back unpainted for now.

2. For the tab, follow my basic directions for shaping bake clay with a cookie cutter, rolling the clay to about a quarter inch thick and using the 1½-inch square cookie cutter. Before baking, trim the piece to fit behind the figure at its bottom.

3. For the base, follow my basic directions for shaping bake clay with a cookie cutter, rolling the clay to about an eighth inch thick and using the round scalloped cookie cutter. Before baking, stand the baked tab on the center of the base and push down to mark the position, then use a craft knife to cut all the way through the base to form a socket for the tab.

4. When the base is baked, make sure the tab fits the socket hole. As needed, sand to fit. Then glue the tab into the hole with epoxy and let it set. For best coverage, place your glue around the top inside rim of the hole, not on the tab. After pushing the tab through, remove excess glue from the bottom.

5. Paint and seal the top and edge of the base.

6. (Optional) When the paint on the base is dry, spread a little white glue or wood glue over the top, and while the glue's still wet, sprinkle mica powder and glitter over it for snow.

7. Glue the figure to the tab.

8. When the glue has set, paint the backs of the figure and tab.

Christmas Train Wreath
Experience Level: Intermediate

Come for a ride on this cheerful holiday train! I promise to get you home in time for Christmas.

The "artificial snowflakes" I added as an optional last step go by a number of different names. To find what you want, try searching online for some combination of "artificial," "fake," or "faux"; "snow" or "snow-flakes"; "glitter," "powder," or "filler"; "decoration" or "crafts."

Don't hang the wreath where it will be exposed to the weather.

Prepare the Wreath Form and Track

1. Cover the wreath form with plastic wrap.
2. Following my basic directions for shaping air-dry clay with a cookie cutter, cut out eleven sections of track from air-dry clay—preferably black—that you've rolled to a thickness of about an eighth inch. Arrange the pieces on top of the wrapped wreath form, bending them by hand to form a circular track and lining up the ends as closely as possible. Hold the pieces in place with T pins or push pins while they dry.

Clay
Air-dry clay (for track pieces and small trees)
Lightweight bake clay (for everything else)

Molds and Cutters
Family Heritage Hometown Train, by Pampered Chef
Train track cookie cutter, by Cookie Cutz
Christmas tree mold, by Wilton
Snowman cookie mold, by OZAOZ
Merry Christmas mold, by Artesão Cookie Molds
Small tree silicone mold

Special Tools and Supplies
18-inch Styrofoam wreath form with flat front
Plastic wrap
1-inch white glitter ribbon
T pins (wig pins)
Push pins (optional)
Fork pins
4-inch needle
1-inch D ring
Artificial snowflakes (optional)

3. After drying, remove the track pieces from the wreath, along with the plastic wrap. Paint the track tops black and seal them, if you didn't use black clay.

4. Wrap the wreath form snugly with 1-inch white glitter ribbon, leaving a length of it free at the end for hanging the wreath. (This free length should be a bit more than *twice* what you want to end up with.)

5. Pass the free end of the ribbon through a 1-inch D ring, then fold the ribbon over and glue the end to the back side of the wreath, fastening it with T pins.

6. Position the track pieces again on the wreath, trimming if needed for fit. Then glue the pieces one at a time to the ribbon with white glue or wood glue.

Make the Other Figures

1. For the train cars, large tree, and Merry Christmas sign, follow my basic directions for molding bake clay in a bakeable mold. For the train cars, use sections of the mold to make an engine, caboose, and two flatbed cars. After baking all pieces, paint and glaze the fronts.

2. For the snowman, follow my basic directions for molding bake clay in a non-bakeable mold. After baking, paint and glaze the front.

3. For the small trees, follow my basic directions for molding air-dry clay. Paint and glaze the fronts, then glue the trees to the top edges of the flatbed train cars.

Assemble

1. Glue fork pins to the backs of the train cars, large tree, and snowman with hot melt glue. Then glue those pieces to the wreath with white glue or wood glue, pushing the fork pins into the Styrofoam. (If you omit the fork pins, follow my basic directions for tack gluing.) To keep the wreath balanced, position two of the train cars on each side of the hanger ribbon.

2. With epoxy, glue the 4-inch needle vertically to the back of the Merry Christmas sign, letting the sharp end extend two inches below. When the glue has set, stick the needle through the ribbon into the Styrofoam and glue the bottom edge of the sign to the wreath. (If you like, you can paint the back of the sign before attaching it to the wreath.)

3. (Optional) Brush the assembled wreath with gloss sealer or thinned white glue and sprinkle it with artificial snowflakes.

Christmas Stocking Hanger
Experience Level: Intermediate

Here's something for an extra festive touch. The kind of stocking hanger I started with is specially designed to be finished with a handcrafted decoration, but other kinds might work as well. Different hangers may require different sizes and shapes of cookie cutter.

My directions are for only one hanger I made, but of course, you're likely to want to make a variety. The deer medallion also seen in the photo was made from air-dry clay with a common silicone mold.

Clay
Lightweight bake clay

Molds and Cutters
Winter Sleigh Ride mold and (optional) cutter, by The Springerle Baker
3-inch round scalloped cookie cutter

Special Tools and Supplies
Stocking hanger for crafts

1. Follow my basic directions for molding bake clay in a non-bakeable mold, then paint and glaze the figure.

2. For the medallion's base, follow my basic directions for shaping bake clay with a cookie cutter. After baking, glue the figure to the base with white glue or wood glue, then paint and seal the base around the figure.

3. Glue the medallion to a stocking hanger, following my basic directions for tack gluing.

Treetop Star
Experience Level: Advanced

I've had this cake topper mold for a long time but have rarely had an excuse to use it. Every time I've looked at it, though, I've imagined it in color as a treetop star. With this project, my fantasy came true!

Only part of the mold was used—the eight diamond-shaped sections of the star. Each section was individually molded, painted, and glued to a supporting wood circle. That was much easier than trying to mold the star as a single piece.

The star is mounted on a Christmas tree topper holder, though for me, that required some adjustment. If your tree is a large artificial one, you might get away with just gluing a wire loop to the star's back.

If you want to make a similar, smaller star, look for Christmas shortbread molds. Many are available in a diamond star pattern.

Clay
Lightweight bake clay

Molds and Cutters
Diamond Star Mold, by Änis-Paradies

Special Tools and Supplies
Unfinished wood circle, ⅛ inch thick,
   5 inches diameter
Christmas tree topper holder

1. Make each of the eight diamond-shaped sections of the star, one at a time, following my basic directions for molding bake clay in a non-bakeable mold. Be sure to get clear impressions of the borders. Use cardboard over the parchment to help support the clay when turning the mold over and to keep the clay from distorting when you separate it from the mold.

2. After baking, glue the sections to the wood circle. Use wood glue *without* tacking so you'll have time to adjust the pieces as needed.

3. Paint and glaze as you like.

4. Attach the star to a Christmas tree topper holder, adapting as needed. (My hardware had a mounting for a ³⁄₁₆-inch rod, but to substitute for that, I whittled the end of a ½-inch square dowel to fit and then glued the dowel to the back of the star.)

Star connecting to tree top holder

Christmas Teatime Wreath

Experience Level: Advanced

This wreath is a whole collection of cookies from different molds and methods, painted and trimmed to resemble real cookies. The ultimate marriage of cookie molds and polymer clay!

I used so many molds and cookie cutters for this one, it would be pointless to identify any but the most important—so give your imagination free rein. (Besides, the Santa-in-sleigh piece at the top was modified so drastically from the mold, it wouldn't do you any good to know what I started from!)

The wreath could be made more easily—and would still be attractive—with fewer types of cookies, if you'd prefer that. Also attractive would be a fir wreath in place of the burlap-covered Styrofoam.

Don't hang the wreath where it will be exposed to the weather.

Clay
Air-dry clay
Lightweight bake clay

Molds and Cutters
Teapot and Cup, by Boston Warehouse
Large Mandala Christmas Tree Silicone Mold, by EmlemsSiliconeMoulds
Santa Face, by Artesão Cookie Molds
Reindeer, by Artesão Cookie Molds
Filigree Wreath, by Kitchen Vixen (for large tarts)
Winter Biscuits rolling pin, by Mood for Wood
Assorted cookie molds and other molds
Assorted cookie cutters

Special Tools and Supplies
18-inch Styrofoam wreath form with flat front
1-inch burlap ribbon
2½-inch wired printed ribbon (for bow)
Modeling clay or impasto
Glitter (optional)
Fake sprinkles (optional)
Fake chocolate chips (optional)
14-gauge aluminum wire
Fork pins
Clear silicone waterproof sealant (tub and tile caulk)

>

Make the Cookies

1. For the Santa face, reindeer, Christmas tree, teapot, and cup, follow my basic directions for molding bake clay in a bakeable mold, then paint and glaze.

2. With aluminum wire, form a brace in the shape of an upside-down U to fit the back of the cup, then glue it on with epoxy. The legs of the brace should extend three inches below the cup so they can be pushed into the wreath. When the glue has set, paint the back of the cup, if desired.

3. For the large tarts, follow my basic directions for molding bake clay in a non-bakeable mold, then paint and glaze. Fill the tarts with modeling paste or impasto, colored with acrylic paint for lemon or chocolate.

4. Make a variety of small, thin cookies—enough to cover most of the wreath—with the Winter Biscuits rolling pin and various cookie cutters in basic shapes. Follow my basic directions for molding a single image with a rolling pin, then paint and glaze the fronts. Attach fork pins to the backs with hot melt glue.

5. For still more cookies on your wreath, use your own choice of molds, cookie cutters, and clay types, then paint and glaze. You can add glitter or fake sprinkles to a cookie by first spreading glue thinly over the surface. Fake chocolate chips can be embedded in air-dry clay before it dries.

Assemble the Wreath

1. Wrap the wreath form snugly with burlap ribbon.

2. Push the ends of the cup's brace through the burlap into the wreath and glue the cup's bottom edge.

Back view of cup, showing wire brace

3. Glue the rolling-pin cookies to the wreath with white glue or wood glue, forming a layer that covers most of the wreath. Push the fork pins into the Styrofoam to hold the cookies securely while the glue dries.

4. As a second layer, attach the larger cookies with clear waterproof silicone sealant (also called tub and tile caulk). Position the teapot so it's pouring into the cup.

5. Make a bow from the wired, printed ribbon and attach it to the wreath with floral wire.

Advent Calendar
Experience Level: Advanced

This advent calendar presents a scene, rather like a miniature room box, framed with numbered drawers that can be filled with candies or small gifts for children.

Traditionally, the drawer numbers stand for the days of Advent, which starts on a different date each year. But if you're not actually observing Advent, you can just treat them as dates in December. On the drawers of this calendar, I've used figures from earring molds to mark the end of each week, and a miniature Santa to mark Christmas Eve. As you wish, omit these or add more! Small charms would also work for this.

My decorations for the Christmas tree in the scene were pretty much based on whatever I had on hand. I just threw everything at it! The important thing is to have fun with it.

The calendar can sit on a table or shelf, or with the addition of picture hanging hardware, can hang from a wall.

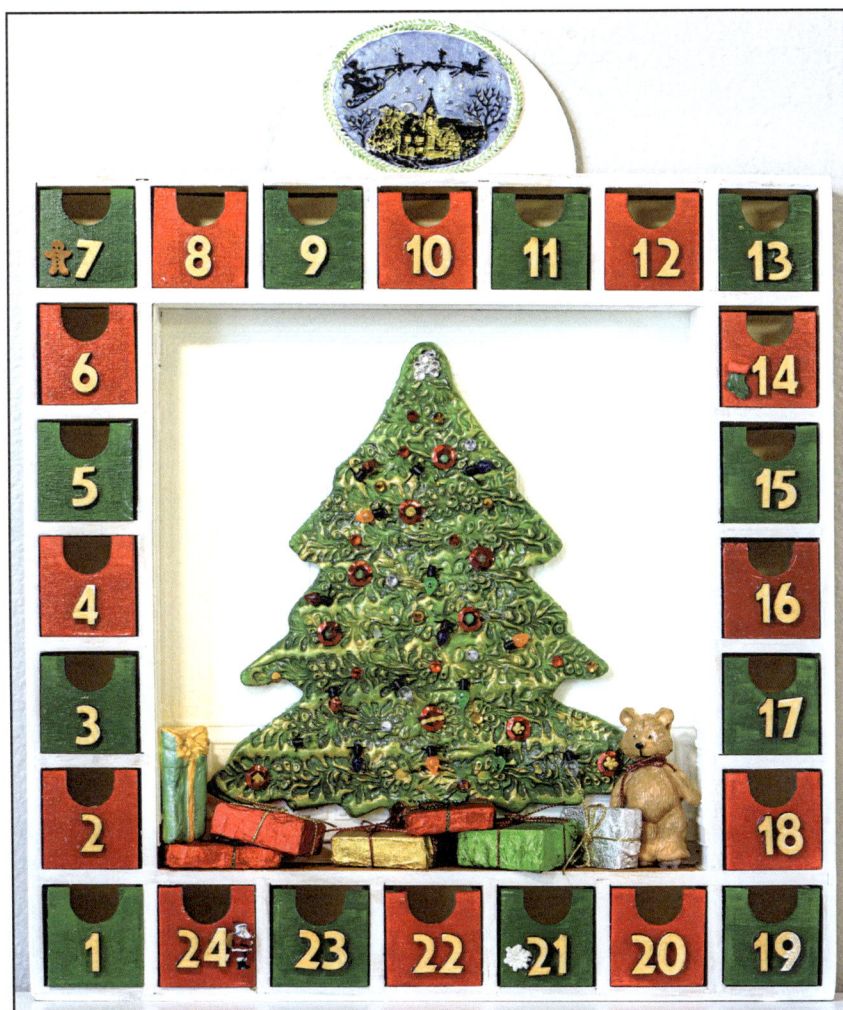

Clay
Lightweight bake clay
Air-dry clay (for teddy bear and molded gift)

Molds and Cutters
Santa Claus is Coming cookie mold, by Änis-Paradies
Mehndi Print Blocks, by Royal Kraft (for tree texture)
Christmas stocking earring mold, by Wild Honey Cutters (optional)
8-inch Christmas tree cookie cutter
Teddy bear silicone mold
Christmas present silicone mold
Earring molds for snowflake, gingerbread man, others (optional)

Special Tools and Supplies
Unfinished wood Advent calendar
Unfinished wood numbers, ½ inch or 15 mm high
Unfinished wood circle, ⅛ inch thick, 5 inches diameter
Dollhouse wallpaper
Christmas lights, by Little Fairy Wishes (optional)
Nail art crystals (optional)
Sequins (optional)
Foil candy wrappers
Thin metallic trim cord, various colors
Metal miniature Santa (optional)
Picture hanging hardware (optional)

Finish the Frame and Drawers

1. Sand the unfinished wood Advent calendar, then paint or stain the frame and drawers. (For the frame, I mixed white acrylic paint with acrylic sealer for a semi-transparent white.)

2. Paint and seal the fronts and edges of the drawer numbers, then glue them to the drawers with white glue or wood glue.

3. (Optional) Make miniature figures with the earring molds and glue them to the drawers.

Create the Scene

1. Cut pieces of dollhouse wallpaper to fit the back and side walls of the room box area and glue them on with white glue.

2. For the Christmas tree, follow my directions for shaping bake clay with a cookie cutter, rolling the clay to about a quarter inch thick. Before cutting out the tree and baking it, stamp the clay all over with the print block.

3. Paint and seal the tree, then glue on the decorations—Christmas lights, nail art crystals, sequins, or anything else you like.

4. Glue the tree to the dollhouse wallpaper with white glue or wood glue.

5. Follow my basic directions for molding air-dry clay to make a teddy bear and a present. Paint and glaze, then glue them in place.

6. For more presents, cut blocks of bake clay and bake them. Wrap them with foil candy wrappers and thin metallic trim cord. Glue in place.

Make the Top Medallion

1. Follow my basic directions for molding bake clay in a non-bakeable mold, then paint and glaze the medallion.

2. Glue the medallion to the unfinished wood circle with white glue or wood glue. The top of the medallion should lie along the circle's edge.

3. Position the wood circle behind the calendar so the medallion appears centered above it, then lightly mark the line where circle and calendar meet. Paint and seal the wood around the medallion above this line.

4. Glue the wood circle in place on the back of the calendar.

Gingerbread House
Experience Level: Advanced

Gingerbread houses from polymer clay are such fun to make and decorate, it's tempting to create a whole village.

The clay is baked right in the gingerbread mold. It takes two of each molding to get all the pieces you need. The walls are glued together with the help of small wood braces, then the roof is glued to the tops of the walls.

The house is painted and decorated only after it's put together. I painted it a warm tan to look like gingerbread cookies, with white trim. Snow is heaped in areas where snow would collect, like the angle between the roof and chimney. Corner joinings are covered by candy canes, and miniature wreaths adorn the front windows. Snow and decorations easily cover flaws and gaps.

Speaking of that village . . . I wound up making two more gingerbread houses with different molds but similar techniques. You can see these too in the photos.

Clay
Bake clay (for the house pieces)
Air-dry clay (for the wreaths)

Molds and Cutters
Gingerbread House, by The
  Pampered Chef
Miniature Wreaths, by
  JennsMOLDSResinClay

Special Tools and Supplies
½-inch square dowel, 12 inches
Small saw or other cutter (for
  dowel)
Wood filler
Acrylic modeling paste or
  acrylic impasto
8 large round beads
Red and green dimensional paint
Glitter or white mica powder
  (optional)

Make the Pieces

1. Following my basic directions for molding bake clay in a bakeable mold, make two full sets of the house pieces. (I ignored the snowman and tree on the mold.)

2. Cut four three-inch pieces of square dowel. On the back of each side wall, center a dowel flush along each vertical edge and glue it in place.

3. Glue your two chimney pieces to each other, back to back. **>**

(Above) Gingerbread house from Stone House mold, by Hartstone Cookie Molds

(Right) Gingerbread house from Gothic Gingerbread Cottage mold, also by Hartstone Cookie Molds

Assemble the House

1. Take your two pieces for the front and back walls of the house and select the best piece for the front. Mark it on its back and set it aside.

2. Center your chimney on the back wall, laying it right over the molded door. Lightly mark the chimney's outline, and also mark on the chimney where the top of the wall meets it. With these markings as guide, glue the chimney to the back wall, following my basic directions for tack gluing.

3. Assemble the walls, using the square dowels as your main gluing surfaces and following my basic directions for tack gluing.

Example of corner bracing, from Stone House (above)

4. Glue the roof pieces on top of the assembled walls, being careful to center the pieces and making sure the shingles point downward.

5. Fill any gaps between pieces with wood filler or acrylic modeling paste.

Paint and Decorate

1. Paint and glaze the house.

2. To make the candy cane molding, form eight thin ropes of air-dry clay, about six inches long, and twist pairs of them together. Cut the ropes to fit the corners of the cottage, with enough room to fit beads at top and bottom. When dry, paint and glaze the twists and beads red and white, then glue them to the house corners.

3. Dab a bit of dimensional paint on the center of each shingle, alternating red and green.

4. For snow, apply acrylic modeling paste or acrylic impasto to roof rims and edges. You can also apply a thin layer of glue to the snow and sprinkle glitter or white mica powder onto it.

5. Following my basic directions for molding air-dry clay, make two wreaths, and after painting, glue them to the front windows.

Index

ANNE L. WATSON is the author of *Baking with Cookie Molds* and *Cookie Molds Around the Year*, which helped launch the modern revival of interest in cookie molds. She has also written popular books on soapmaking and housekeeping, as well as many novels and children's books. In a previous career, she was a historic preservation architecture consultant. Anne lives with her husband and photographer, Aaron Shepard, in Bellingham, Washington. You can visit her online and ask her questions at

www.annelwatson.com

Also for cookie mold lovers . . .

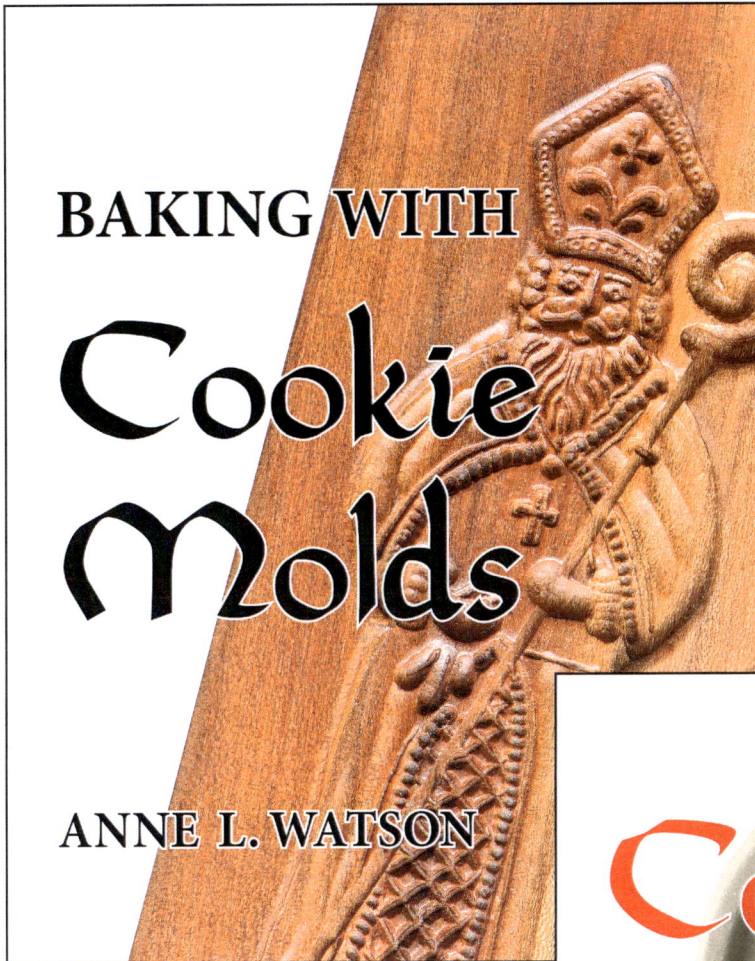

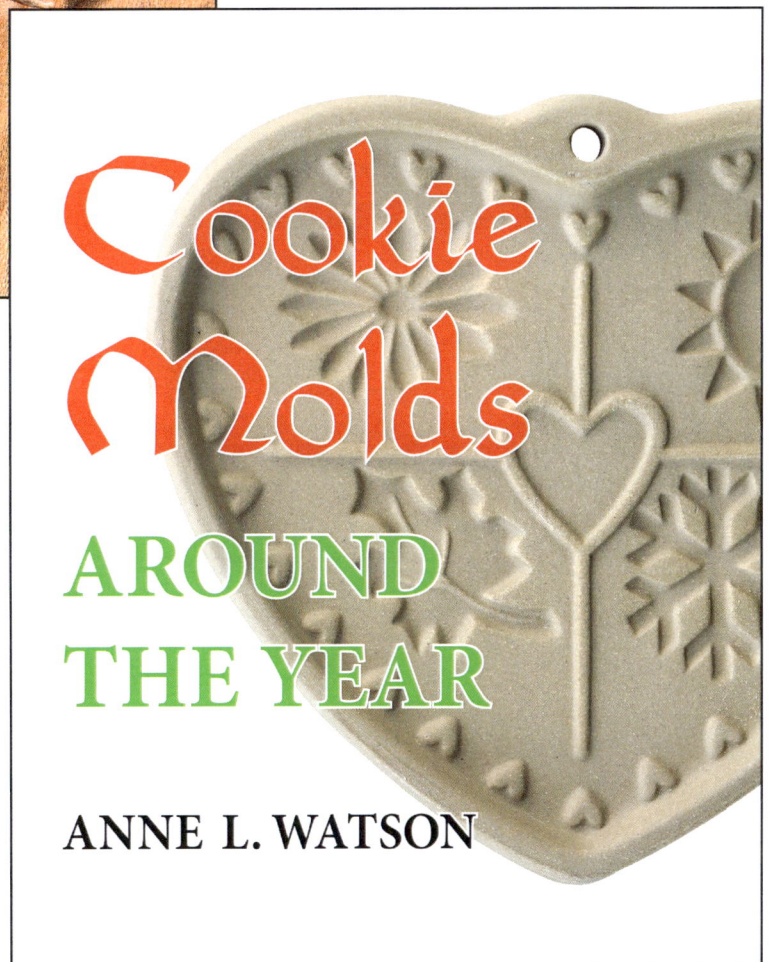

9 781620 356272